Praise for *Mothering & Daughtering*

"*Mothering & Daughtering* has been deeply meaningful to us. Sil and Eliza have given us practical tools and wisdom which transformed our relationship and deepened our bond during the challenging teenage years. This beautifully written book is fresh with creative ideas and is a gift to all mothers and their teenage daughters." EILEEN FISHER, designer and SASHA FISHER ZWIEBEL

"If these challenges between mother and daughter are a generational thing, Sil has surely broken the pattern with her own daughter."
JANE FONDA
Actor and author of *My Life So Far*

"This is the best guide I know for navigating the challenges and beauty of the mother-daughter relationship. Sil and Eliza's work is profound, essential, and revolutionary." GENEEN ROTH
#1 *New York Times* bestselling author of *Women Food and God*

"*Mothering & Daughtering* is a gem, a precious insight into the growth of mothers and daughters, and into the honesty and cherishing of each other."
MARION WOODMAN
Jungian analyst and author of *Addiction to Perfection*

"Mother-daughter conflict during the teen years is neither inevitable nor healthy. There's another way. Read this book and learn how to keep your mother-daughter bond strong and healthy for a lifetime."
CHRISTIANE NORTHRUP, MD
Author of the *New York Times* bestsellers *Women's Bodies, Women's Wisdom* and *The Wisdom of Menopause*

"What you hold in your hands is more than a book—it's a lifeline to mothers and daughters who want to move through the teen years with a real, loving, and lasting relationships. Both Sil and Eliza believe that as girls grow away from childhood and toward adulthood, they actually want and need to stay close to their mothers; and that mothers also want and need closeness, even as they help their girls find their own voices and spread their wings. In this guidebook for a new kind of mother-daughter relationship, Sil and Eliza challenge the stereotype of the broken bond between mother and daughter. They provide inspiration and tools honed from their own experience, and from the hundreds of moms and girls they have helped in their workshops. If you are a mother or a daughter who wants to navigate the teen years side-by-side, please read this book." ELIZABETH LESSER

Cofounder, Omega Institute and author of *Broken Open: How Difficult Times Can Help Us Grow*

"Finally someone talks about the complex and amazing mother-daughter relationship in an authentic way. Our mothers are our superheroes, our nemeses, our role models, and our cautionary tales. It's so nice to read someone who gets that and writes about it with great respect for the paradox. In this powerful book, Eliza and Sil Reynolds offer mothers and daughters the only kind of wisdom really worth giving—a reminder that the big secret to a resilient bond is nothing less than love. Their voices intermingle authentically and eloquently, a model for us all of shared, intergenerational leadership and the power of courageous communication." COURTNEY E. MARTIN

Author of *Perfect Girls, Starving Daughters* and *Do It Anyway*

"What I love most about this book is how honest and down-to-earth Sil and Eliza are about themselves and their relationship. Girls and their moms will find comfort and companionship from two people who are themselves walking the path of the often complex mother-daughter dynamic—and who offer strategies and wisdom that will help all of us become more aware, authentic mothers and daughters." RACHEL SIMMONS

Author of *Odd Girl Out* and *The Curse of the Good Girl*

"This book is a precious gem that I wish had been around for my daughters' adolescences. Sil and Eliza give a timeless gift to mothers and daughters to help them deepen their love and understanding of each other before, during, and after adolescence. Moms who dread the thought of raising their daughters in their teen years will value this lifesaver of practical wisdom. Daughters who are in the midst of figuring out who they are separate from their mothers will appreciate Eliza's advice on how to have a supportive relationship with their mothers without constant fighting. Even though my daughters are now wonderful women, I want to share this book with them and look forward to the conversations and new understandings that this book encourages." NANCY GRUVER

Founder of New Moon Girl Media

MOTHERING & DAUGHTERING

MOTHERING & DAUGHTERING

KEEPING YOUR BOND STRONG
THROUGH THE TEEN YEARS

Sil Reynolds, RN, & Eliza Reynolds

sounds true
BOULDER, COLORADO

Sounds True, Inc.
Boulder, CO 80306

Published 2013

Cover and book design by Rachael Murray

Printed in the United States of America

Library of Congress Cataloging-in-Publication Data

Reynolds, Sil.

  Mothering & daughtering : keeping your bond strong through the teen years / by Sil & Eliza Reynolds.

    p. cm.

  ISBN 978-1-60407-885-5

  1. Mothers and daughters. 2. Parent and teenager. 3. Parenting. 4. Daughters.
  I. Reynolds, Eliza. II. Title. III. Title: Mothering and daughtering.

  HQ799.15.R49 2013

  306.874'3—dc23

  2012037251

Ebook ISBN: 978-1-60407-946-3

10 9 8 7 6 5 4 3 2

MOTHERING

Sil Reynolds, RN

CONTENTS

For Peter

Acknowledgments

I AM INDEBTED TO MY beloved friend Francie White for inspiring me to lead mother/adolescent-daughter workshops in the first place. Wendy Mallet was my wonderful first coleader. Eliza and I joined forces a couple of years later, when Elizabeth Lesser invited us to teach our first Mothering & Daughtering weekend workshop at the Omega Institute. Our book concept is her brainchild, and my gratitude to Elizabeth for the gift of being able to actually teach the subject I feel passionately about—mother-daughter relationships—is immense.

Nan Gatewood Satter, editor extraordinaire, never faltered in her belief in and support of our vision. Nan trusted her intuition and led us to our sensitive and savvy agent, Cynthia Cannell. I am in awe of these two women, who, with equal brain hemispheres ablaze, have brilliantly led us through the maze of the publishing world, as well as through the equally challenging world of writing a book.

Old friend Greg Zelonka wholeheartedly recommended us to Sounds True, and by such personal extensions of faith, our book proposal made it into the hands of the wonderful Jennifer Brown. Although we knew of the reputation of Sounds True publisher Tami Simon and her appreciation for important new work, I wasn't fully prepared for the pure delight of knowing her in person. She has a razor-sharp mind and a huge heart. The extraordinary wisdom, care, and enthusiasm of the entire Sounds True staff—Chantal Pierrat, Jennifer Holder, Tucker Collins, Wendy Gardner, and Rachael Murray, the very talented and flexible designer—made our work with this book both seamless and joyful. They are a testament to Tami's vision and values.

Haven Iverson, editor-in-chief and goddess extraordinaire, often understood our book better than we did. Her insight and mothering of this book helped me fall in love with the writing process all over again as I edited the final manuscript.

I am so very grateful for the time, wisdom, and thoughtful feedback the readers of my manuscript gave me: thank you to Anita, Annie, Eileen, Elizabeth, Jackie, Peter, and Molly.

Carol Donahoe has been our cheerleader at the Omega Institute, and Geneen Roth has been a dear friend and a brilliant mentor for decades.

To my beloved village mothers who helped me (and Peter) raise Eliza— my gratitude for their love and support and mentoring of Eliza is beyond words: Abbey, Annie, Barbara, Edit, Eileen, Elizabeth, Eve, Gina, Jackie, Jeanne, Kali, Linda B., Linda K., Livia, Lorraine, Natalie, Patrice, and— mothering from afar—my most beloved Molly.

I also have my beloved village daughters to thank. They have "daughtered" me with their vision, creativity, humor, courage, and love: Baila, Corey, Corina, Ella G., Ella S., Grace, Gwen, Lola, Lucia, Miranda, Morgan, Sarah, Sascha, Sasha, and Sophia.

Thanks and love to Phyllis Luberg for everything.

This book was inspired by our work with the wise mothers and marvelous daughters who come to our workshops. All names and stories have been altered so that they are unrecognizable. But the inspiration and gratitude remain.

My mother and father are models for living an enthusiastic and honorable life.

My husband, Peter, has been my rock through the process of writing this book, and he has given me essential guidance. And even though I have doubted my mothering skills, he never did, and he is an outstanding father to our Eliza.

My utmost gratitude and love is for Eliza, who daughtered me with exquisite tenderness and tact as we wrote this book together. Eliza, you are my greatest pride and my deepest joy. My cup runneth over.

PREFACE

OUR MOTHER-DAUGHTER WORKSHOPS AND THIS book came into being because I wanted to help mothers access their intuition and their emotional intelligence so that they can then use these tools confidently when they need them most. Too many mothers find their intuition to be dormant or buried for far too long, just as it was for their own mothers before them, and so it is passed on along the matriline, a generation or two at a time. But if there is anything I have learned along the way, it is this: the vast, nearly universal majority of mothers already know how to raise their adolescent daughters just fine. They carry the answers within them, ready to rise to their daughter's need, like Venus rising on her half shell. This knowledge has gradually become very clear to me over the thirty years that I have worked as a family nurse-practitioner, psychotherapist, and mother-daughter workshop leader. But at the same time, sadly, has come the twin truth that many of these same mothers, for various familiar and widely shared reasons, have real difficulty accessing their answers.

Mothering my adolescent daughter awakened my intuition, enhanced my emotional intelligence, and brought me to life—rather, it brought me to living my *own* life instead of the one prescribed by my parents or my ancestors or the culture at large. Eliza's adolescence forced me to face my own unfinished adolescence and to actually grow up, so that I could become the adult she needed in our relationship. And it was my mother's intuition that helped keep our bond strong through Eliza's teen years. This Mothering side of *Mothering & Daughtering* reflects what I have learned, both personally and professionally, along the way.

I acknowledge C. G. Jung and three pathfinders—Marion Woodman, Mary Hamilton, and Ann Skinner—who furthered Jung's work by applying it more accessibly to the particular psychology of women. Without their decades of work, our mother-daughter workshops would not have been born, nor would I have found confidence in my mother's intuition through my daughter's thoroughly challenging, and fascinating, teen years.

SIL REYNOLDS
April 2013

INTRODUCTION

The Mothering & Daughtering Path

Adolescents transform—they do not abandon their relationships with their parents, particularly with their mother . . . only if they are unable to work within the relationships they so clearly value . . . only then does the adolescent see her task as one of separating from her parents.

—TERRI APTER

"I REALLY DON'T KNOW HOW I'll make it through the next few months with my daughter Alexa," says Susan, "much less the next few years. I'm suddenly like the enemy. I need help. *We* need help. *Fast.*"

Once we're out of her daughter's hearing, Susan tells me that the bond between her and her daughter seemed to unravel overnight. Fourteen-year-old Alexa is now challenging almost every decision Susan makes, every boundary she establishes, and every curfew she sets—and with attitude. Hurt, confused, and increasingly unsure of herself, Susan sees her daughter slipping away from her.

Susan had visited our Mothering & Daughtering website and discovered that the next weekend workshop for mothers and their teenage daughters was two months away—if you didn't count the workshop that had started that very night, that is. So that same afternoon, Susan cajoled her daughter to the car and drove one hundred miles to Rhinebeck, New York, home of the Omega Institute. The pair arrived unannounced at the registration area, looking isolated and worn-out. Susan asked, "Could you squeeze the two of us into the Mothering & Daughtering workshop? *Please?*"

Part of Susan's confusion was that her friends (along with plenty of experts) had been reassuring her that Alexa's withdrawal was perfectly normal—teenage girls need to separate from their moms, they said, and it's usually through some kind of ritualistic, protracted battle of wills. "But don't worry," the well-meaning friends and experts continued. "This battle will strengthen your daughter, and someday she'll forgive you, both for the tough love you tried to assert in between her incoming texts and for being so impossibly embarrassing and weak as she fought her way toward independence." Finally, one day in the distant future—or so goes this piece of CW (that's "conventional wisdom")—she will return as an equal, and her battles will have prepared her to take on her own teen girl when the time comes, just as your battles with your mother, perhaps, prepared you to take on your teen girl.

Does this situation sound familiar? If you are locked into a clash of wills with your preteen or teenage daughter, or if you fear the prospect of getting into one, you are not alone. In fact, you are bunkered alongside hundreds of thousands of other moms in a zeitgeist that seems to accept unnecessary mother-daughter battles as inevitable, while offering no support for genuine closeness. In the Mothering & Daughtering workshops that my daughter, Eliza, and I lead together for preteens, teens, and their moms, we meet countless mothers who are exhausted by their efforts to act as positive role models and to assert healthy limits on their daughters' activities—whether on the Internet, with friends, with dating, at the mall, at parties, or even at school. Just as telling, we find that their daughters are also exhausted by the endless, ongoing negotiations that are going on at home while they seek to form a separate identity and their own way of moving in the world.

It was by monitoring our own ups and downs as we went through Eliza's teen years, as well as by gathering lots of data through our work together over the past five years, that Eliza and I came to believe that this clash of wills works for neither mother nor daughter. Neither really wants to become a hardened survivor of a years-long battle that she will have to hope to someday get beyond. Instead, along the way, Eliza and I discovered that there is another, much easier, and more natural way to travel this potentially tumultuous path through teenage life, one in which having a strong, mutual, and flexible bond with each other can provide the support both mother *and* daughter need for the journey. This built-in mutual support is available to moms and daughters at any time and lies at the ready, right beneath the challenging, turbulent, and often scary surface of everyday contemporary life. We've found that it exists despite the various histories of divorce, trauma, and everyday poor communication that mother-daughter pairs so often bring to our workshops. And we've seen that moms and their teen girls really do want to help, rather than battle, each other through this challenging phase—a phase that can be supportive, healthy, and generative. So how do we find this different way of being together? How do we work with a more positive model that embraces the profound, lifelong mother-daughter bond *now?* How do we do this throughout all phases of life? And, finally, as Susan and Alexa asked us so desperately: How do we find it *fast?*

Many good books offer tools and strategies to help parents like Susan manage conflict with their teenage daughters more easily and effectively. In part, this is what the Mothering side of this book is about. Under the layer of practical strategies, though, is a deeper, less effortful source of help that I want to offer you—one that encourages you to cultivate a capacity within yourself that *already knows* how to parent your adolescent daughter well. This capacity is *intuition,* an innate capacity and a highly attuned sensibility that we all have. Our current culture, which is increasingly juvenile and combative, does not encourage us to develop this valuable sensibility—one that requires us to take pause, "listen" within, and consider our behavior. This Mothering side is designed to help you recognize your intuition, to cultivate it, and to use it as a guide as you mother your daughter. I am encouraging you to become more *conscious* of your intuition as you mother.

Simply put, conscious mothering is mothering with an increasing awareness of our unconscious beliefs and behaviors, especially those beliefs and behaviors that are not useful or effective as we raise our daughters. We must be careful, however, that we don't take on this practice of increasing our awareness as a burden, as one more thing we have to add to our to-do list in the already-overwhelming role of mothering our adolescent daughters. Instead, increasing our awareness of how and when to use our intuition will make this task easier, because it will improve communication and strengthen the mother-daughter bond. Please note: Conscious mothering is not perfect mothering. It is a daily practice that does not consider perfection a desirable or obtainable goal. My own consciousness and confidence grew as I mothered my teenage daughter very imperfectly. Through this process, I landed on four cornerstones of the Mothering & Daughtering approach:

1. **You and your daughter have a bond for life.** It is together, as a team, that you can make this bond positive and enduring. If you are both committed to staying connected through your daughter's teen years, you are more than halfway there. This book aims to give *both* of you the tools that will help you find that commitment and stay connected.

2. **You, her father or your partner are the most important people in your daughter's life.** Her relationship with her father is for another book, but here is what is true about her relationship with you: she longs to rely on you, to share her private matters with you, to learn how to love her feminine body and self, and to have her new and emerging identity as a woman lovingly mirrored back to her.

3. **Your adolescent daughter actually wants and needs you to stay at the center of her life.** It is important that you are conscious of this, even if she isn't. It is by you staying reliably at the center of her life, as a steady and mature presence, that she can find her way to healthy independence as a true adult.

4. **When the mother-daughter bond is strong, the challenges of raising an adolescent daughter tend to invigorate, rather than exhaust, a mother.** A strong mother-daughter bond is the foundation from which good communication happens, trust grows, and limits are honored. Did I mention that it is also much more fun?

I want to pause here and consider number 3 in more depth. It may surprise you that your adolescent daughter wants and needs you to stay at the center of her life. I am sure that you are hearing a lot about the damage that "helicopter" mothers can do, and you have probably been getting a pretty strong message from the conventional wisdom that you should mother from a safe distance. There is no doubt that true helicopter moms are extremely anxious about their child's successes and failures and, as a result, are overinvolved and have a harder time than others in following the moving, tidal shoreline between where they end and their emerging daughter begins. It is not a stretch to guess that a helicopter mother (or father) may not have found enough fulfillment in her own life and that she is living her "unlived" life through her child. Her hovering can impede her child's growth.

It has been my experience, however, that helicopter mothers are rare. With just a little coaching, the majority of mothers I have worked with know how to be at the center of their daughter's life and how to be vividly involved without overstepping the line into the sovereignty of their daughter's selfhood. And most mothers are able to have regular access to the intuition and wisdom that are needed to know the difference between the two.

Although their mood swings and ambivalent feelings make it challenging for us mothers to remember it, our teenage daughters crave our everyday guidance and loving support in their lives. One leader in this field of hands-on adolescent parenting is Dr. Terri Apter of the United Kingdom, whose research has shown this to be true. I will be discussing Dr. Apter's work on the relationships of mothers and their adolescent daughters further in chapter 1.

More than likely, it has not escaped your attention that there is a powerful undercurrent pulling your daughter away from you and toward her peers. You have probably heard from others—be they friends, family, or experts—that this pull to her teen peer group as the new central structure in her life (her new family) is a normal and necessary step as she exerts her independence. But I am recommending that you rethink this notion. A peer group is not a parent, and its unreliable herd thinking makes the intimacy and authenticity your daughter needs at this time hard to find. I have observed that some of our daughters are determined to bring themselves up on their own or are looking to their peers for the emotional support and guidance they need through adolescence. Yet, an adolescent peer is simply not developmentally capable of providing the steady and mature counsel that our daughters need from adults, and it will cause our daughters tremendous anxiety if their peer group is their primary source of counsel and support.

Your adolescent daughter is becoming an individual—both separate from and connected to you. Psychological and neurobiological research has demonstrated that she needs you to be *more* present, not less, as she seeks a new identity. I will share about this research, as well as the stories of some of the mothers and daughters in our workshops who had been stuck in battle but who are now reconnecting and thriving. Let's be clear: A thriving relationship includes tension and disagreements, both of which are grist for the mill. However, this "grist" does not have to be destructive to the relationship. Instead, you can and should use the tension and disagreements to help the relationship grow, rather than erode. Even if she seems to be saying otherwise, your adolescent daughter needs and wants to be close and connected to you. She needs to depend on you in order to become independent, she needs healthy attachment to you in order to become secure, and she needs to be guided and protected by you as she establishes an authenticity that will give her the confidence she needs in life.

It has been in experiencing this mothering and daughtering path through Eliza's adolescence and by teaching workshops together that we have come up with our working definitions of *mothering* and *daughtering*. These definitions have guided us on our own path, and we trust you will find them very useful as you travel yours:

Mothering: Raising your daughter to become herself

Daughtering: Being active in your relationship with your mom
so that she knows the real you; balancing your independence with
a dependable bond as you grow into your true self

In raising your daughter to become herself—the authentic person she was born to be—your intuition is more important than any advice you receive from friends, family, and experts. Advice can be incredibly helpful, but because each daughter has her own personality and comes with her own unique set of characteristics—such as a strong will, introversion, or emotional sensitivity—your inner guidance system can make all the difference. I believe that nothing works as effectively as your intuition in meeting the challenges that your individual daughter offers you "on the ground" and in the moment.

In chapters 1 and 3, I encourage you to pay attention to this inner guidance system of yours and to learn to recognize your daughter's natural, though not always obvious, attachment instinct. Your intuition will also help you know how to encourage your daughter to balance her independence with a dependable bond with you as she grows. And the more adept you become at listening to your intuition and reading your daughter's attachment instinct, the easier your mothering path will be. If you don't already have the strong bond with your daughter that you both need, I offer strategies for reestablishing your naturally close relationship. If you do have it, I offer strategies for keeping it that way.

In chapter 2, I encourage you to use your emotional intelligence to explore your relationship with your own mother as a way of becoming more conscious about the way you are mothering your teenage daughter. What have you inherited from your mother (and she from her mother) that you can embody and carry forward? What patterns have you inherited that you may want to heal so that your daughter will not have to carry them into the future? Was your mother able to mirror (really "see") you and contain (really "hold") you so that you could grow and thrive? More important, are you able to do this for yourself?

What follows from these inquiries is that some of the issues you have with your mother may be affecting your relationship with your daughter. You don't have to work out these issues with your mother in person, as she may not be alive or she may not be open to or comfortable with working on your relationship. As you will learn in chapter 2, you can heal many of these issues internally without your mother being present.

I've found it very challenging to raise my teenage daughter in a culture that encourages her to look externally—instead of internally—to find her value and self-esteem, and to look to her body, her grades, and her material possessions to find happiness and identity. How can we be true to our daughter's unique expression and encourage her to fully express her *soul*—I love that word—in a competitive culture that insists on standardized testing and standardized beauty? How can we mothers meet the challenges of raising a preteen or teenage daughter so that her life belongs to *her* and is not a performance for others? *Mirroring* and *containing* your daughter—two key mothering skills that I will describe in depth—will help you find her at any time and guide her safely out of the treacherous territories of comparison, performance, and perfectionism. Learning these skills, which are clearly outlined in chapters 4 and 5, will come naturally to you as you practice them.

In chapter 6, I focus on the everyday reality of what it takes to find the energy, determination, and support we mothers need in order to hold on to our daughters while we are maximally challenged by our overscheduled lives. *What's a mother to do?* is the operative question as I discuss sex, discipline, money, and how to prevent a technological takeover in your home by providing regularly scheduled family time and a "village" that helps you raise your daughter.

Because mothering and daughtering is a joint activity, Eliza joins me in a shared chapter (chapter 7) between mother and daughter. It is the same chapter she carefully guides your daughter toward from the very first page of her Daughtering side. In this shared chapter, we help you put your heads and hearts together so you can design your own plan to continue to deepen and strengthen your bond. If this bond is hard for you to find and needs to be recovered, Eliza and I will show both of you the way back to a working relationship. Thus, we have designed this book to work from wherever you are—whether you are already thriving in your relationship or merely surviving and feeling hopeless and disconnected from your bond. In the shared chapter, Eliza and I will "chat" with each other as we guide you through conversations and exercises (don't worry, you can interrupt us), until you and your daughter are both satisfied that there is a path forward together. In fact, you might want to think of this whole book as a private communication workshop, with you, your daughter, Eliza, and me all working together toward a common end. If your daughter wants no part of this "workshop," and you are the sole reader, you absolutely can improve your communication and strengthen your bond even without her reading the Daughtering side or the shared chapter.

Before you proceed into our shared chapter 7, however, it is essential that you read Eliza's Daughtering side of our book as an accompaniment to my Mothering side. There is much we can learn from our daughters if we listen well, and I think you will find Eliza's daughtering perspective a worthy and refreshing companion to my mothering perspective. And what a valuable entryway into your daughter's world! I must confess that with all my talk about the value of a daughter's voice, I wasn't fully prepared for how much I would learn from Eliza as we wrote—how substantial, necessary, and insightful her daughtering work *really* is. I ended up editing out quite a few things I'd written for you on my side because Eliza has a livelier and fresher perspective—and there were many times I found that her perspective offered a viewpoint that is much more effective at helping readers embody this work. This process was both thrilling and humbling, just like the mothering process.

In particular, Eliza provides both daughters and mothers with some excellent guidance for honing our intuition, growing our emotional intelligence, and learning to accept and love our bodies. You'll also find a number of places in the Mothering chapters that refer you to specific material in the Daughtering chapters for insight into how our girls tend to think differently from us about a given topic. The Daughtering chapters will engage your daughter in the intense issues of the day—and of *her* day—which no doubt include (consciously or not and either by obsession or omission) her issues with you, her mother ground.

Your girl is probably taking you for granted much of the time. More than likely, she is way more focused on her social life and her updates on Facebook than she is on you. Or maybe she is consumed by a book series or a sport she feels passionate about. Undoubtedly, she is concerned with homework and how she can manage her own overscheduled life. She is probably worrying to some degree about fitting in with her peers, about how she looks, about friends who are engaging in risky behavior (or about her own risky behavior), and about her latest crush or intimate relationship.

Because Eliza is just coming out of her teenage years, she knows what is occupying your daughter's inner and outer life. As a mentor to your girl, Eliza will encourage your daughter to express herself authentically—something that is hard to do in her current conformist peer culture. Eliza also wants your daughter to know that you will, and can, be her best guide as she navigates this culture in search of a new identity, and that growing into her own identity does not mean she needs to reject you. On the contrary, Eliza shares her own experience of staying connected to me—even as she resisted me and disagreed with me—and how our strong bond felt essential to her, and even "cool" (after some very "uncool" moments), during her adolescent years. She makes it clear that your daughter yearns for and needs your support. Eliza is also committed to helping your daughter recognize her longing to be close to you—even if her longing has been usurped by peer relationships. It was by my staying steadily involved in Eliza's life, in spite of her very natural resistance, that Eliza became clear that she needed my support. By working hard at not taking her resistance personally and hanging in with her no matter what, I helped her learn that my support was essential. She learned that she needed me as a reliable, emotionally mature adult. And yet I had to remember, again and again, that emotional maturity does not mean that we do not make mistakes in our relationships. It does mean, however, that we must take responsibility for those mistakes and repair them. Eliza and I emphasize in each side of our book how important it is to repair after a "rupture," whether that repair comes in the form of a heartfelt apology or getting to the bottom of a misunderstanding and clarifying each other's points of view—or both!

Eliza and I have made our way through the trials and tribulations of her adolescence (approximately ages eleven to twenty-one) to find ourselves in a relationship that we both feel good about—one that is intimate, strong, and satisfying. I am grateful that our challenges were not exacerbated by divorce, trauma, or serious financial stress, as these days it is hard enough to raise an adolescent daughter well under the luckiest of situations. Those who manage with these challenges are doing the hardest work of all, and my admiration for them is vast.

My own becoming a student of this "mothering work" through my mentorship with the Jungian author and analyst Marion Woodman was essential to our good outcome. But I must tell you that I did some very "heavy lifting," especially when Eliza was fourteen, fifteen, and sixteen. She had an older boyfriend (two years older—an eternity at that age!) and was hanging out with older friends who were driving. There were many limits and boundaries that needed to be negotiated, and Eliza was frankly a burden to be around for many a day. Her moodiness had me walking on eggshells, and each day brought new emotional upheavals and challenges. But the more I made a practice of imagining that those eggshells were, in fact, solid ground, tread on by many a fine mother before me, the more I got into my stride. Trusting my gut—my intuition—was a crucial part of finding this kind of confidence in my body and "on the ground."

Now Eliza has her feet firmly planted on the ground of young adulthood; she is self-reliant, whole, and happy in herself. "Whole" does not mean she doesn't struggle—it means that she has a healthy sense of herself and that she has the tools to communicate well and negotiate the challenges that come her way. We both know that she is going to be fine, and more than fine: she will thrive. Part of her strength comes from our bond. Human beings are wired for deep connection, and when the bond between parent and child is strong, we are stronger as individuals. Part of her strength also comes from her bond with her father. In some ways, it feels incomplete to write this book and not discuss Eliza's relationship with her father and write exuberantly about the syncopated coparenting he provided. His relationship with Eliza during her teen years was close and abiding, and their bond is wholly different in nature and rhythm and value from my relationship with her. She is in many ways "a father's daughter," which itself is a fascinating topic! But in this book, we are about mothers and daughters and the many psychological and cultural issues that swirl about the challenges for both. So here we simply give a shout out to her father and to all great fathers—I trust they will understand, and as many men would, not mind at all that we are leaving it at that.

I also trust that you mothers with more than one child will understand that as a mother of one daughter, I cannot share an experience of keeping the bond strong with more than one child. Although you and I don't share the joys and challenges of sibling relationships, I believe we have much in common, no matter how many daughters (and sons) we have and love. And I believe you will find that our Mothering & Daughtering approach is consummately useful, no matter how many children you have.

These days, Eliza and I deeply enjoy each other's company, and we talk often about all manner of things. We agree and disagree, and we hear each other out; we respect each other, and we laugh a lot. I am still in a mother role, of course— I always will be. But it's a role that continues to evolve. What I notice now is that Eliza "mothers" herself well. Her dependence on me during her adolescence created a healthy independence, just as her attachment to me created a genuine inner security. She has learned that her love of dance and books and authentic friendships feeds her soul, even though she does not use the word *soul* very often. ("That is your word, Mom.") And she feels passionately about sharing her journey with your daughter.

It is Eliza's and my hope that this book will help you and your teenage daughter leave—or better yet, never even enter—a battlefield that serves no purpose. We know that you and your daughter will be challenged as she grows, but we are certain that these challenges can be the constructive building blocks of a strong mother-daughter bond. We hope you will find inspiration and a shared language from the Mothering & Daughtering approach, where the very process of working through your conflicts together will help you build the foundation necessary for a deep and enduring relationship, a relationship that can be a source of support, joy, and love throughout your lives. Starting right *now.*

1

A Daughter's Instinct

Our society is so topsy-turvy that we may actually come to value the child's willingness to separate more than her instincts for closeness.
—GORDON NEUFELD AND GABOR MATÉ

LATELY, FOURTEEN-YEAR-OLD ERICA HAS BEEN moodier than usual. In fact, according to her mother, Susanna, Erica has been *far* moodier than usual. Gone are the days when Susanna's sunny girl delighted in seeing her mom after school to chat away about her day. Now, when Erica returns home, Susanna often tries to extract something—just a scrap, a little anecdote, a small hint of what is the cause of Erica's distant and dark presence. But the more questions Susanna asks, the more irritable and monosyllabic Erica's responses become. What had once been an afterschool ritual of connection has become an afterschool ritual of dissonance and separation, one that usually ends with Erica interrupting her mother midquestion in order to head to her bedroom and connect with her friends online. Once so sure of her mothering skills, Susanna has begun to lose confidence in her ability to get through to her daughter.

Your adolescent girl's words (or lack of words), her behavior, and her body language may be very hard to decipher. But no matter where she is on the mood continuum, I can guarantee that she wants to connect with you. Even though almost every sign and every word may be communicating her displeasure with you, she desperately wants you in the center of her life. Chances are, she is barely conscious of this need. She is, after all, subject to the same cultural bias that we mothers are, which says she is supposed to be beyond the need for mothering as soon as she can find her friends on Facebook. And since she has come to realize that you, in fact, are not perfect (a realization that may have been more painful for her than you know), it may seem plausible to her that her equally challenged peers—who aren't perfect either, but at least they *understand* her—are now more reliable and accurate mirrors by which to live. In her ambivalent state, her natural desire for closeness to you may be so hard for you to discern that it may take every ounce of patience you have to hang in there with her. Often, however, embedded in the chaos of her frustration and acting out, the hidden call will come. It is the test: "Be there for me anyway! No matter how much I talk back or tell you to go away!"

Susanna was having a hard time reading her daughter's attachment instinct, this hidden call behind Erica's behavior, and she was having an even harder time remaining patient and loving. She was becoming increasingly testy in her interactions with Erica and was afraid that she might lose her ability to remain the adult in the relationship.

NOT TAKING HER BEHAVIOR PERSONALLY

We are not saints; we are mothers. Like saints, however, it is probable that when we first set out on our paths, we had no idea of the challenges we'd face or of the patience and fortitude we'd be required to muster. And right now, as the mother of a teenage daughter, you are being called upon to muster large amounts of patience and fortitude for yet a while longer. To the degree that you can remember to do this when your frustrated adolescent saves her worst behavior for you alone, your path will be that much less difficult. I am certain that you have what it takes for you to hang in there with her—as long as you can depersonalize her behavior and remember that she wants and needs to have a good relationship with you. Understanding adolescence will make it so much easier for you to not take her behavior personally.

Some refer to adolescence as a birth. And yes, it is a very long delivery, with a lot of contractions for both mother and daughter. But if we mothers can get our bearings straight and our support system established, then we can help make our adolescent daughters' growth process as fascinating and as awe-inspiring as the changes we watched in her infancy, or when she was a toddler taking her first steps, or as she put together her first sentence, or, for that matter, when she had her first tantrum. In fact, a toddler's tantrum can be instructive (though admittedly exhausting) if we understand its purpose (to let off the steam of frustration) and if we don't take it personally. If we handle the tantrum of our toddler with a calm and loving detachment—though every parent knows that this is far easier said than done—then by the tantrum's end, our little girl can come into our strong and steady arms, relieved that her world has not fallen apart. We see that we can provide her with the emotional antidote for her growing pains, and it can be incredibly rewarding.

The same is true for parenting during adolescence. Handling a teen "tantrum" with a calm and loving detachment means that we must find an even deeper reserve of wisdom and compassion than we once mustered for the obviously healthy and necessary (even sometimes amusing!) tantrums of our toddler. Although a teenager can be almost as impulsive as a two-year-old, the former is much larger and has many more words at her disposal as she has it out with us. But the impulse and the function of this tantrum is the same as it is for the toddler. As long as our daughter is not threatening our safety as she lashes out, we can learn that she is being affected by some painful truth and needing to transgress acceptability for now. Thus, it may not be the best approach to confront her in the heat of the moment. The prefrontal lobe of our brains, which is responsible for impulse control, is considerably more developed in us than it is in our adolescent daughters. We literally have the neurological tools to stay detached and to not take our daughter's behavior personally, and to know that it is best to work out any conflict after the storm has passed.

These days, creating a good relationship with an adolescent requires more than compassion for her growing pains and an understanding of her adolescent brain. We also need to understand the society in which we live—a society that makes it harder and harder for us to stay connected to our daughters. In the midst of our overscheduled lives, our daughters are being wooed out from under us by unhealthy images, jaded or empty values, mind-altering substances, and even "friends" who are not true friends. If I sound like a holier-than-thou goody-goody, let me assure you, I'm not. But I *am* concerned for all of our daughters, and it's clear to me that we can use our mother's intuition, our common sense, and the wisdom we have acquired over the course of our lifetimes for the benefit of our daughters. To what better purpose could our experience be applied?

Along with our experience, it is extremely useful for us to understand adolescent development within the context of the topsy-turvy culture in which our daughters are growing up. Let's begin by equipping ourselves with an understanding of our adolescent daughters' psychological development and their attachment instinct. If we understand the basics, we will have taken the primary steps in learning to keep her close (if we still "have" her) or to bring her back to a connected relationship (if we have "lost" her). We will also be better equipped to not take her behavior personally if we know that it is normal for our daughter to resist us and question us as she seeks to form her identity.

THE PSYCHOLOGICAL DEVELOPMENT
OF ADOLESCENT GIRLS

Perhaps no person has contributed more to helping us understand an adolescent girl's behavior and "reframing her resistance" than the psychologist Carol Gilligan. With the publication in 1982 of *In a Different Voice: Psychological Theory and Women's Development,* a new psychological theory was born—one in which girls and women are seen, heard, and understood. Through her research, Gilligan inspired us to look at what had been regarded as women's weaknesses—that is, their emotional expression, their empathy in relationships, and their need to stay connected in relationships—and see them as human strengths. One way that adolescent girls show their need to connect with and be guided by their parents is through resisting and rejecting. But they are not resisting and rejecting us; they are resisting and rejecting old modes of communicating that are no longer useful for their (or our!) growth. At the root of your daughter's resistance is a longing for honesty and authenticity in her relationship with you.

The same year that Gilligan published *In a Different Voice,* Jungian analyst Marion Woodman published *Addiction to Perfection,* the first of a dozen books that she would write in the years that followed, all of them redefining women's psychology from a Jungian perspective. It was in *Addiction to Perfection* that Woodman first elaborated on Jung's concept of the human need for healthy psychological and spiritual containment. Where Jung had left off, Woodman picked up, defining a woman's need for psychological and spiritual containment as being distinct and different from a man's. In particular, Woodman explored the emotional wounds that are unique to women and that come through the matriline. One of Woodman's greatest gifts to our understanding of women's psychology is her work and research on the potential for women to heal emotionally, at any age, through skilled and loving containment by another and within themselves.

Gilligan, Woodman, Terri Apter, and other psychologists and educators have continued their research on women and girls over the years. Books such as *Meeting at the Crossroads: Women's Psychology and Girls' Development* (Gilligan), *Women, Girls, and Psychotherapy: Reframing Resistance* (Gilligan), and *Altered Loves: Mothers and Daughters During Adolescence* (Apter) have further elucidated our understanding of the psychology of women and girls—and of mothers and daughters. What the researchers discovered was that girls' psychological development was very different from that of boys. Apter elucidated Nancy Chodorow's reworking of the female Oedipal phase conceived by Freud:

> The enormous influence Chodorow's reworking of the female Oedipal phase had [in *The Reproduction of Mothering*] is a result not so much of a reconsideration of the way in which a girl desires her father, or a phallus, *but the way in which she remains connected to her mother as she forms her identity*—in particular her gender identity, her sense of herself as a female. We can see how, for a girl, the "relational self" dominates a distinct self, and leaves women more inclined to seek, need, and value attachment to others (emphasis added).[1]

In essence, research was leading us to a new and more accurate model of adolescent development, one that demonstrated that an adolescent *needs* relationship with her parents in order to achieve a healthy individuality. It is through this relationship that she can hope to get validation for a new sense of self. In particular, a girl looks to her mother for affirmation of this self, often through resistance and complaints. If we mothers understand our adolescent daughter's natural attachment instinct, we will be better able to "read" her confusing cues and ambivalent feelings toward us as the call that it is—the call to be seen and heard in a new way, but also as the call for us to stay close.

Our Preteen Daughter's Attachment Instinct

In the preteen years, our daughters are likely to be giving us the most delightful and overt signals of their desire to remain attached to us. This period of cuddling, imitation, and sharing may and should be without bounds. Yet, at one of our recent preteen (ten-to-twelve year olds) Mothering & Daughtering workshops, one thoughtful mother, named Carrie, admitted to our circle of mothers something that I see as a disturbing sign of our time. She shared that she was starting to feel self-conscious about how affectionate she and her eleven-year-old daughter, Louisa, are in public. "I feel as if I am being judged by others for having a close relationship with Louisa! She's in sixth grade, and she still likes to hold my hand. Sometimes she climbs into my lap. I know that my friends and family don't think we are normal, and I am beginning to believe we aren't." Carrie discovered that she was not alone. Barbara confessed, with some embarrassment, that her ten-year-old daughter, Elena, still climbs into bed with her at night on occasion. Barbara wondered if there was something wrong with Elena and wanted to know if she was damaging her daughter's psychological development by allowing Elena to cuddle with her when she feels frightened or upset. Would it be healthier to encourage her daughter to tough it out in the dark? Elena's father certainly thought so. Annette, the mother of twelve-year-old Linda, told us that Linda was content to hang out with her and her husband most Friday and Saturday nights. Although Annette and her husband were delighted with Linda's company, they were worried that she wasn't interested in having sleepovers with her friends or going to the boy-girl parties that her peer group had recently been organizing. Although Annette could see that Linda was a happy and well-adjusted girl, she wondered if there was something wrong with her daughter because she did not care to socialize with her peers in this way. Annette asked me if Linda was normal.

Normal means "conforming to a standard: usual, typical, or expected." Thus, I had to answer that no, her daughter was not normal. However, because we are living in a topsy-turvy society, we mothers need to turn things over a bit for ourselves to discover our own truths about our bonds with our daughters, and question whether "normal" is the goal to which we want to aspire. That day at our workshop, I informed these mothers that although their daughters' behavior may not be the norm these days, or "normal," it is totally natural—that is, it is *instinctual.* If we trust their instincts, our preteen daughters will let us know exactly what they need, and they will show us that they know their own needs just as well as they did when they were younger and were seeking comfort and closeness. Your own preteen daughter may have a limited desire for physical contact with you—every girl is different. But if your preteen girl has a desire for physical contact and proximity—as many do—it can and should be welcomed. Just as when our daughters were toddlers and clung to us for dear life before boldly setting out to explore the world, so too as a preteen, they may literally be clinging to us as they prepare to make the leap into the teen years.

Our Teen Daughter's Attachment Instinct

Things change, though, for many of our daughters as they cross a perceived threshold into the larger world. In a year or two, Louisa won't be climbing into Carrie's lap as she did when she was eleven; Elena will grow out of wanting to get into bed with her mother when she is afraid at night; and Linda will not be spending most Friday and Saturday nights with her parents. The sudden cessation of many preteens' openly loving habits can cause a mother to feel as if her own world has turned upside down. Many mothers feel that they have been cast as the source, rather than the solution, to their girls' problems of the moment and that they are being treated as "The Enemy."

But don't be fooled. Just because your teenage daughter is less physical with you and wants to hang out with her peers more than ever before, and just because she is giving you some (or a lot) of attitude, this does not mean she doesn't want to be close to you. She wants to be as close and connected to you as she ever was, but now sometimes it is from a comfortable distance. Some of my best bonding time with Eliza during the teen years was from one room away—me involved in a work project, and Eliza humming away as she did her homework, with the door open between us. "Close and connected" is a state that can mean as many things as there are mother-daughter relationships, but you will know it when you have it. By checking in with your mother's *intuition*—a kind of tuning fork in your body that I will discuss in chapter 3—you will be able to assess your relationship with your daughter and make adjustments when necessary. It has been my experience that learning to listen to your gut is the first step in learning how to keep your daughter close and safe during the teen years.

The mothers in our preteen workshops are often bracing themselves for what they are afraid is just around the corner—an inevitable and protracted battle of wills, a painful separation, and an unworkable relationship with their soon-to-be teenage girls. Many of these mothers had painful experiences growing up as teenagers, constantly at odds with their own mothers. At these workshops, there is often a sense of urgency in the air, a desperate hope that history will not repeat itself. Since I was a very angry and rebellious teenager myself, I understand just how miserable the teenage years can be for a mother and daughter, and I can empathize with these mothers' fears. I caused my mother anguish on a regular basis, I am sorry to say, and she watched helplessly as I pushed her away.

When I gave birth to a daughter, I heard the never-ending predictions of irresolvable conflict during the teen years. Throughout Eliza's childhood, people would say with a hint of sadism, "Just you wait until she's a teenager!" Their warnings frightened me, even though I could not imagine my adorable baby, my sweet six-year-old, or my thoroughly confident and delightful nine-year-old being anything but the sweet, confident, and delightful child that she was. How could this exquisite loving just *stop*?

When Eliza did become a teenager, sometimes a friend or an acquaintance would ask me with concern or even pity, "How's it going?" I knew they expected me to roll my eyes and unload. I began to find the question a little insulting—not just to my girl, but to all teenage girls. I had certainly put my mother through hell, but is this a universal and permanent cultural condition? The answer need not be yes. If my mother had understood that my anger toward her was a plea for support and connection, things may have been very different for us when I was a teenager. There is a possibility that I would not have looked to my peers for the guidance and refuge that I needed from an adult.

COMPETING FOR YOUR DAUGHTER'S ATTACHMENT

Our daughters are being wooed more and more actively—and at an earlier age than ever before—by what psychologist Dr. Gordon Neufeld has called *attachment competition*. In this case, that competition comes from our daughters' peer group and the Internet. Many of the mothers in our preteen workshops are distressed that their daughters are already rejecting their advances, including greetings, hugs, and kisses that had been so welcome just months before. In our Mothering & Daughtering teen workshop for mothers and their thirteen- to fifteen-year-old daughters, mothers who see their daughters orienting themselves to their peer culture are in the majority. Frequently, these mothers are alarmed at how quickly they are "losing" their daughters. It is more challenging than ever to know how to stay involved in our daughters' lives.

The first steps in reclaiming them (or not losing them in the first place) are straightforward and linear. If we can keep an eye on our daughter's social schedule and her time on Facebook and the Internet, and if we set *reasonable but firm* boundaries for her (not just reasonable, but firm; not just firm, but reasonable), we have accomplished a huge part of the task. Chances are your intuition will guide you most of the way in determining what is reasonable and firm, as well as in deciding how to handle the regular negotiating that you are having with your daughter over limits. My husband and I had to stay true to our values and to the limits we both felt comfortable with (I will discuss this more in chapter 6). Suffice it to say that Eliza's refrain was often, "But everybody else is doing it!" We demonstrated reasonableness by listening respectfully to her entreaties for more social freedoms, and we demonstrated an equal firmness by setting appropriate limits that took into consideration her age, her safety, and our values.

As a child and beneficiary of the increased freedom of the 1960s and 1970s, the irony of hearing myself put forth such a plan is not lost on me. But I, too, hope to have learned the ultimate lesson of finding a balance with things. Once we are successful at finding some sort of balance with the competition for attachment from her peers, we must then be true to our aim and establish regular time and space to be together with our daughters so that we may nurture our bond. Attachment competition is everywhere, and some mothers must literally schedule their daughters into their appointment calendars. I am recommending that you do whatever it takes to have quality time with each other on a daily basis. Your relationship with your daughter will not thrive if you don't make this happen. Quality time doesn't have to mean an hour-long talk in a private setting, though those are nice, too. Quality time can be something as simple as cooking dinner together, doing errands together, a good talk during the ride home from school or an activity, or helping with her homework. In fact, doing projects together (instead of a planned meeting time "to talk") is usually the most conducive environment for spontaneous and meaningful conversations with teenagers. If you are divorced and sharing custody of your daughter or if she is at boarding school, then daily texting, phone calls, and face time on Skype will help you keep your bond strong. I recommend phone calls and face time on the computer over texting—hearing the human voice and seeing the human face are better ways for us to find our human bond.

CREATING YOUR OWN WORKSHOP

Even when you carve out time and are successfully keeping her peer group and the Internet at bay, you still may be mightily challenged in relating to this emerging person. "Nurturing" your relationship with your daughter may involve a great deal of intense communicating and arguing. Your teenage daughter is bound to push you away. She is not rejecting you—you are far too important to her for that. *She is merely rejecting an outdated mode of relating to you.* This is why it is absolutely crucial that you not react reflexively to behavior you don't like. Instead, look beneath the behavior to discern what she is trying to say. Her pushback is feedback, and you may not be listening as deeply and carefully as she needs you to. She is growing up fast, and she is in search of a new identity and a role model who can help her navigate her stormy waters. She desperately needs you to respond in new ways as she searches to find her voice and her true self. It is likely that you are the safest person with whom she can work this out. It is your task as her mother to stay committed to finding time together and to working through this new stage of your relationship.

Many of the mothers in our workshops have had to dig deep to find the determination and persistence required to get their thirteen- to fifteen-year-old daughters to come away with them for two-and-a-half days. They share stories of pulling their daughters—with a few daughters literally kicking and screaming—to our workshop weekend. Because Eliza and I know full well that these mothers are competing with peer attachments in order to have some precious time away to bond with their daughters, we schedule our workshop on Mother's Day weekend. This way, the mothers have the attachment edge when they tell their daughters they want to spend a weekend away for a Mother's Day present.

It is remarkable to watch how easily skeptical teenage daughters can melt back into their mothers' arms, literally and figuratively, over the course of a weekend. Yes, we offer creative strategies and fun games for bonding—as well as plenty of time for the girls to hang out with Eliza and each other discussing non-mom-related issues of importance to them. But the secret to the success of our workshops is far simpler: When a mother and her adolescent daughter get away for just a weekend, without the distractions of their everyday lives and the competing attachments that are at every turn, they do what mammals do best. They bond. They rediscover each other. They often fall in love again. They don't necessarily need a workshop, though the community support is wonderfully biased in favor of bonding. What they need is time together, without distractions, to find each other. Nature, in all her eminent wisdom, helps us reconnect when we mothers and daughters carve out the time and create the space to trust and follow our attachment instincts. Therefore, it is extremely important that you—mother reader—know that you do not have to attend one of our workshops in order to recharge or rekindle your connection with your daughter. Eliza and I have written this book together so that you and your daughter can create your *own* "workshop."

A big part of creating your own workshop, in addition to carving out time to spend together on a regular basis, is learning to read and trust your daughter's instinct to stay close to you. Resistance to you and your guidance doesn't mean she wants you gone. On the contrary, she needs you to acknowledge and appreciate her independent thinking. It is developmentally appropriate for her to resist you and your guidance; she is finding her own thoughts and feelings, which need to be separate from yours. Imagine how satisfying your relationship with your daughter could be if every time she appeared to be resisting you, you reframed her resistance for what it really is: a search for her true self. Her instinct is to be independent and to remain connected to you *at the same time.* You must encourage her in both of these endeavors.

THE RESEARCH EVIDENCE FOR
ATTACHMENT PARENTING IN ADOLESCENCE

But you will be challenged—and not just by your daughter. You may also get the message from family, friends, and educators that you are hovering. I know that my parents watched with some concern as they observed my hands-on approach to mothering. Their parenting style with me and my brothers in the 1970s, for better or worse, was very laissez-faire. Whenever we get looks or feedback or even jokes about our hands-on parenting style (some call it *attachment parenting*), we need to consult our own experience and intuition for guidance: Wouldn't we, as teens, have loved such a reliable and connected relationship with our mothers? Today, backing up our experience and intuition is strong evidence from emerging research in family psychology and child development that supports all our efforts to stay close to our daughters, even in adolescence.

Over the past fifty years or so, psychological research has led to the creation of a new model for viewing our independent selves in relationship to others—in particular, to our families. For example, *family systems theory,* a theory originated by psychiatrist Dr. Murray Bowen, offers therapeutic techniques as well as a philosophy that searches for the causes of a behavior, not only in the individual but also in interactions among the members of a family. According to Dr. Bowen, individuals cannot be understood in isolation from one another, but rather as part of an emotional unit that is a family system. We are all interconnected and interdependent, and how we relate to everyone in our family system—our spouse, our parents, and even our siblings—can have a profound effect on our children.

In addition, current research in the quickly expanding field of neuroscience offers convincing data that parents and children grow together and affect each other's neurobiology throughout their entire life span—a finding that emphasizes the need for healthy *relations* within the family. Children—and that means teenagers, too—don't go through developmental changes by themselves; parents change with them. A mother and her daughter both grow and change *together,* though certainly the adolescent daughter's growth is more dramatic (in more ways than one).

As a daughter grows from infant to child to teenager, we slowly but surely allow her greater sovereignty. Dr. Apter points out that unfortunately, our mothering role is often seen in all-or-nothing terms: we raise a daughter, and then one day, we are supposed to let her go. We need to look to a newer version of our role based on a much, much older version of what is possible: an attachment bond between mothers and daughters that remains strong throughout our entire lives. Until our daughters are in their early twenties, it's likely that we need to be the holders of this vision.

While they are teenagers, our girls may not have the emotional maturity or clarity to even imagine a lifelong bond or to articulate their very real attachment needs.

Attachment parenting, a phrase coined by pediatrician William Sears, is a parenting philosophy based on the principles of attachment theory in developmental psychology. According to attachment theory, the child forms a strong emotional bond with caregivers during childhood, and this bond has lifelong consequences. Sensitive and emotionally available parenting helps the child form a secure attachment style that fosters a child's socioemotional development and well-being. Over the years, attachment parenting has been co-opted, to some degree, by proponents of controversial techniques, and thus it is sometimes misunderstood and criticized.

Attachment Parenting International's (API's) Eight Principles of Parenting were laid out for the care of babies:[2]

1. Prepare for parenting
2. Feed with love and respect
3. Respond with sensitivity
4. Use nurturing touch
5. Ensure safe sleep, physically and emotionally
6. Provide consistent and loving care
7. Practice positive discipline
8. Strive for balance in personal and family life

Although these *strategies* for parenting will change from infancy to adolescence, the *fundamentals* remain the same. In addition, upon looking at this list, it should become obvious that we are being guided to parent in the instinctual behavior of our ancestors. It is important to remember that our infant's—as well as our adolescent's—attachment instinct is her biological bond to us. Attachment is a biological system developed through evolution to protect not only our children but also our bonds with our children.

A unique attribute of humans has been to extend this attachment and parental investment through adolescence. Brain scientists and social anthropologists now deem this strategy as being responsible for our long-term survival and success as a species. Furthermore, the human brain isn't fully developed until we are in our midtwenties!

I am sure that one reason attachment parenting has become so popular in our culture is that we have lost touch with some of our most basic instincts—instincts that came naturally to our ancestors. We have to reclaim those instincts and perhaps relearn them. As you can see from these eight principles, attachment parenting is not radical parenting. Rather, it is natural parenting. Although this list is more focused on the needs of an infant or child, every principle is a useful reminder to us as we raise our adolescent daughters.

Unlike the research data on babies' and children's attachment needs, data on teenagers' attachment needs hasn't made it into mainstream understanding. The attachment parenting philosophies of Dr. Sears and Dr. Harvey Karp have made these wise pediatricians household names. Sears's invaluable work put the school of attachment parenting on the map of parenting literature in the 1980s, and Karp's attunement techniques have helped millions of exhausted and distressed parents learn to tend to their babies' and toddlers' needs and make them the happiest babies and happiest toddlers on the block. But what knowledge can fill the void that still exists for most of us about how we can continue tending to our children's very real emotional needs into the teenage years?

Dr. Terri Apter's research on mothers and their adolescent daughters teaches us that the kind of emotionally attuned parenting described by Drs. Sears and Karp is quite similar to how we can effectively mother our teenage daughters.[3] This does not mean we need to carry our adolescent daughters around with us in baby slings! It *does* mean that we need to safeguard and nourish strong connections with our children. According to API, "Attachment parenting challenges us to treat our children with kindness, respect, and dignity and to model in our interactions with them the way we'd like them to interact with others."[4] That's *exactly* what we want to do as the parents of our teenagers.

The fundamental principles of mothering well don't need to change when our daughter becomes a teenager. In 1990, Dr. Apter's *Altered Loves,* a groundbreaking book devoted to understanding mother-daughter relationships during adolescence, was published to critical acclaim. Backed by her meticulous research regarding mothers and their adolescent daughters in action, she makes this essential point in her 2004 book *You Don't Really Know Me:*

> Rather than asking how daughters become independent and
> separate, it is more to the point to ask how daughters retain their
> attachment to their mothers as they themselves grow and change.
> The "task" of adolescence is not to sever the closeness, but to alter it.[5]

On the other side of adolescence is an altered love between mother and daughter, and this love can be as deep and as satisfying as it ever was, perhaps even more so. I notice this in my relationship with Eliza, who now meets me in the middle of our exchanges with an attunement and respect that rivals mine. I find that I don't linger in mourning over the loss of all the other Elizas that have come and gone along the way—that yummy baby, the thoroughly sweet six-year-old, the bold and self-possessed nine-year-old, the marvelous and moody teenager, and all the Elizas in between—because I now find myself in relationship with a mature, compassionate, and self-confident young woman who is still my daughter. She and I are both nourished by this new woman-to-woman rapport, with all the richness and change that align with it.

TRANSLATING YOUR DAUGHTER'S RESISTANCE

To arrive at a place where you have a mutually satisfying and adult rapport with your daughter, you will first have to learn how to translate your teenage daughter's attachment cues along the way. Dr. Karp named the toddler's language *Toddler-ese*. Let's name our teenage daughter's language *Teenager-ese*.

If we understand that there is a positive reason for why she is pushing us away or being moody or picking a fight, we will be able to transform a potentially negative interaction with our daughter into an opportunity to connect. Consider this kind of interaction as a kind of martial-arts encounter—I don't mean a kung-fu street battle, but rather a daily practice session of an ancient and honed dance, one where we meet changing energies with solid purpose. Since you are the adult in this martial-arts dance, it is likely that you have earned quite a few more belts than your daughter-partner has. You may not have earned these belts in the family in which you grew up, but think about the belts you have earned in other intimate relationships. If you remain conscious of the fact that deep down she *always, always* wants to connect, then you will recognize your daughter's moody cues as a signal of her need, not as a rejection of you. You will know in the moment how to make the most effective and strategic mothering-as-a-martial-art move.

So, what is the positive reason your daughter is trying to push you away? She is in the process of trying on a new identity, which means she is trying to become her own person, with her own thoughts and her own will and her own feelings. She needs to push you away to some extent so that she can figure out *who she is.* But we never should leave our girls alone to figure this out on their own or solely with the help of their peers. When Susanna and I spoke about Erica's moods and their awkward interactions in the kitchen after school, I pointed out that she still had an opening with her daughter. After all, every day after school, Erica was still plunking herself down in the kitchen where Susanna was working. She only went upstairs to her computer after Susanna nervously asked too many open-ended questions. Open-ended questions such as, "How was school today?" can be the kiss of death in a conversation with a teenager! A great mothering martial-art dance move is to ask a few indirect questions, such as "Would you like a snack?" or "Did you hear that Grandma called last night?" And, of course, to let there be silence.

Susanna admitted to me that she could feel intimidated by Erica and that Erica's surly behavior made her feel anxious. I remember feeling the same way at times with Eliza. I felt as if she were possessed by the spirit of my teenage past and that instant karma had come to get me! I gained confidence, however, as I remembered the constant energy shifts that Eliza was navigating, including an identity that was shifting on a weekly (or daily) basis with dramatic intensity. That helped me remember that I did not have to take Eliza's resistance personally. If you can remember that trying on new identities is your daughter's part of the martial-art dance, then you might find it easier to do your part of the dance—that is, meeting her where she feels she actually is. At first, you may find yourself at least a step or two behind (I certainly was); but then you will learn the art of catching her energy and shifting it without seeming to.

Part of mastering our new mothering martial art might be in addressing our daughters' shifting energy and moods without confronting them. Understanding that Eliza's shifting energy and moods were part of a natural counterwill in her was a huge revelation for me. *Counterwill* is a term first coined by the Austrian psychoanalyst Otto Rank, and in his book *Hold On To Your Kids,*

Norman Neufeld describes it as "an instinctive, automatic resistance to any sense of being forced." This is different from *will* as we usually know it—that is, a will concerned with doing whatever is necessary to achieve our goals, for example. When we talk about a child being strong willed, we usually mean that we are experiencing her counterwill and that she *perceives* that we are trying to coerce her into doing something else. Dr. Neufeld explains that counterwill is an instinct directly linked to our relationship with our children and that this instinct is meant both to keep our children safe (because sometimes people will try to coerce them and it is good for them to know how to "fight back") and to help them develop their own independence over time.

Understanding that counterwill in your daughter is actually an instinct for growth and survival can change how you look at her resistance and can lead to more successful and less stressful mothering. For example, when confronted with counterwill, you might now find yourself smiling inside while maintaining a steady respect for the drama of what she feels. It will help, no doubt, if you can remember your own experiences at her age. Recall and connect to your own adolescent moments of confusion and fear and counterwill, as well as your craving at that time for a steady, knowing, and all-forgiving presence. Remembering that feeling can help guide you in these moments with your own teen girl.

Once you really understand that your daughter still needs you, you will be inspired to find new ways of connecting with her. You will be able to welcome the ongoing negotiations of rules and values that come with mothering an adolescent daughter as an opportunity to connect and reinforce your relationship. Mothering your teenage daughter can feel so creative and meaningful that you will be energized by the task and by the healing it can bring to your own wounded adolescence. If you were a teenager who swore you'd do better by your own daughter—listen to her better, criticize her less, trust her more—then knowing that you are making good on your old commitment will be a hugely nourishing gift to your psyche, as well as to hers.

Our culture would have us believe that it is unhealthy and selfish to hold on to our teenage daughters, and that other adolescents somehow know best what the emerging young women we've raised need in each moment to thrive. But at the risk of sounding fundamentalist in my convictions, I believe that holding on to our society's ineffective and outdated ideas of independence and maturity is irresponsible. Instead, I believe that we can and must respond to our teenage daughters' very real need for the mother-daughter bond to stay strong.

You will certainly be challenged to find that balance between staying close to her while giving her the room she needs to grow, just as your own mother may have been (or may still be) similarly challenged. But you will surely find this balance with your daughter if you make use of the love and attachment that is already the foundation of your relationship with her and if you keep listening deeply to her often-mystifying attachment cues. Before you know it, you will find yourself sitting across from a self-assured and loving young woman—a woman who is also your daughter.

2

A Daughter's Inheritance

The task which her own mother may have failed to perform, she must perform. That is the new consciousness, the giant leap, the healing in her own life which she is being called upon to incorporate.
—MARION WOODMAN

IT SEEMS THAT MOTHERING ALWAYS has one more challenge to offer, and so I offer you one more idea to consider: in order to be effective "martial-arts moms," we need to stop feeling that there is something wrong with us if we have not successfully completed emotional and psychological separation from our own parents—in particular, from our own mothers. Even if our own adolescence remains spectacularly incomplete, we can still create and maintain a healthy intimacy with our own daughters, an intimacy that is fortifying and nourishing for her. We can still be a mature model and presence for her. So before we go further in talking about building your bond with your daughter, I feel that it is important for you to reflect on your relationship with your own mother.

Here is an example: In a workshop, we are just beginning a part of the day in which I sit alone with the mothers. Joanna, a schoolteacher who has come with her fifteen-year-old daughter, Bethany, is tearing up. "How did I let this happen?" She tells us how her "once sweet girl" has utterly changed in the past six months and how Bethany now spends most of her time talking to or texting her boyfriend on her cell phone. Joanna tells me that whenever she tries to set limits with Bethany for phone time with her boyfriend, Bethany goes "ballistic."

Joanna is at a loss as to how to reconnect with the daughter she once knew so well, as well as how to discipline her without further alienating her. It is evident to me that at this very moment, a troubling new perception is bubbling up for her. With an out-of-body voice, she tells us that at Bethany's age, she had subjected her mother to exactly the same harsh treatment. "I shut my mother out and put her through hell, and we still hurt each other even today. I was sure that I could escape this with Bethany." The pain and regret she is feeling are palpable. "How did I pass this on?"

Also in our group is Beth, a nurse and single mother, who relies on her own mother living nearby to take care of her twelve-year-old daughter, Miranda, after school. Beth and her mother have never been close; she describes their relationship when she was a teenager as "a nightmare." Beth feels undermined as a mother as *her* own mother seeks to "mold" Miranda into the "perfect" granddaughter. "How can I possibly help my daughter be herself when my mother wants her to be anything *but* herself?"

Soon after, Sally weeps as she confesses that she recently struck her fifteen-year-old daughter, Rebecca, who had been screaming at the top of her lungs during an argument. "I lost it," Sally tells us shamefully, still in a state of shock. Sally has started therapy so that Rebecca will never suffer at her hands again, just as she had suffered at her own mother's hands. Sally wants our workshop weekend to be part of the reconciliation she is having with Rebecca. I remind these mothers—and all of the mothers who attend our workshops—that just as we come to the weekend as mothers, we also, without exception, come as *daughters*.

Not all workshop mothers are in the kind of crisis situations faced by Joanna, Beth, and Sally. Many have solid relationships with their daughters, and they have come for preventive strategies as they brace themselves for what they are sure will be an inevitable clash of wills. Even mothers who are faring well are afraid—and some are terrified—that they will repeat or fall into the same agonizing or stultifying relationships they had (or may still have) with their own mothers. They never imagined they would be standing at this particular precipice with their own preteen or teenage daughter. As we go around our circle, each mother shares why she has come, and many are surprised by the immediacy and intensity of their feelings about their relationships with their mothers. After all, this was supposed to be a workshop about relationships with their *daughters!*

But we mothers are all daughters, of course. So let's take a look at the psychological and emotional legacy that your mother has passed on to you. If this legacy includes pain and misunderstanding, I urge you to heal as much of it as you can so that your relationship with your daughter has a greater opportunity to thrive. If this legacy is a positive one, you can choose to pass it on.

In chapter 3, I discuss what recent research in neuroscience is teaching us about the two hemispheres of the brain. In the past couple of decades, there has also been a research focus on the limbic, or relational, part of the brain. This research has taught us about mirror neurons and appropriately attuned contingent parental responses, which I also discuss in chapter 3. This research has given us the scientific tools to assess much of what we have long known intuitively: that *love matters,* not just in the development of an infant but also in the raising of an adolescent daughter. The loving attention that we give our daughters will influence their future relationships as well as the circuitry in their brains.[1] Remarkably, love is even capable of creating new circuitry in our adult brains. We mothers can actually learn to regulate and heal our own brains and nervous systems by choosing loving relationships and by treating *ourselves* in a loving manner.[2] In doing so, we directly affect the emotional intelligence and psychological health that we pass on to our daughters.

Ask yourself what you may have inherited from your mother and what, in turn, she may have inherited from her mother, and so on down the line. In other words, what is your emotional legacy? Where do you still feel pain in your relationship with your mother? Are there ways in which you did not feel seen or held? Try to name some of those pieces. (If you don't feel pain in your relationship with your mother and if you have felt seen and held by her, this is a wonderful emotional legacy that you are passing on to your daughter!)

What do you want to pass on to your daughter, and what do you *not* want to pass on? Do you feel as if you have the tools to determine these things? If not, are you losing your confidence as a mother now that your daughter is approaching or has arrived at adolescence? If *love matters* as we parent, what is love, and how do we find it when our teenage daughters are pushing us to our limits? Where do we find the patience? The wisdom? The emotional intelligence? The stamina? Becoming more conscious about how we want to mother our teenage daughters is a process, as you are surely discovering. There are no easy answers, and there is no one way to do the job "right."

Joanna, Beth, and Sally all said they are confident in the job they do in the world, and yet their maternal emotional legacies often render them feeling helpless and ineffective as they mother their teenage daughters. Many of the mothers who come to our workshops seeking support and advice are also working professionals—teachers, attorneys, nurses, physicians, psychotherapists, spiritual leaders, and corporate executives. They can run a board meeting, teach a middle-school math class, fight a case in court, or preach a sermon. But many of these very same professionals confess that they are at a loss as to how to manage their relationships with their teenage daughter. I have found that exploring the conflicts they had—and, in fact, may still have—with their own mothers can help them mother their daughter with increased clarity and confidence.

HEALING YOUR EMOTIONAL AND PSYCHOLOGICAL LEGACY

I remember reading the book *My Mother/My Self* by Nancy Friday in the 1970s, when I was in my twenties. This groundbreaking work examined the psychological complexities of the mother-daughter relationship through interviews with hundreds of women. Friday articulated and explored the idea that women inherit a maternal psychological legacy, and she encouraged women to examine, even challenge, their relationships with their mothers in order to discover who they were. Even for young feminists, this felt like a radical act at the time—to challenge the ways in which our mothers had raised us felt as though we were challenging the sacredness of motherhood itself! For us, defenders of women, it was hard not to feel as if we were betraying the very women to whom we owed the most—our mothers—by critiquing their methods of mothering. For many of us, the inquiry itself, not to mention the discussion, felt taboo.

Now, even three or four decades later, honestly discussing how we were raised and the inherent conflicts and challenges of the mother-daughter relationship can still feel off-limits to many. Part of the reason that Beth feels so trapped in her relationship with her mother is that she and her mother never developed a language for communicating. Beth feels confident as the head nurse in a cardiac care unit, yet she never learned how to speak up to her mother. Her mother raised her by dominating her, and even now, Beth feels as though her mother is overstepping her boundaries—this time in the way that her mother oversees Miranda.

Afterward, when I asked Beth what was in the way of her communicating directly to her mother now that she is an adult, she responded, "I feel disloyal when I think about telling her how I really feel. She spends hours every week picking up Miranda and taking her to her afterschool activities while I'm at work. But I know her influence is not good for Miranda; sometimes I feel it's even toxic. Something has to change." I agreed with Beth that something had to change, and I offered some matrilineal healing advice: "It's hard to feel disloyal to your mother, but you have to look at being loyal to Miranda. That may be one way you can turn this around."

Over the rest of the weekend, I watched Beth's confidence grow as she integrated the idea of changing the direction of her loyalty on the motherline. She came to see that speaking up to her mother was not actually being disloyal—it only felt that way after a lifetime of not voicing her own truth in that relationship. When she thought in terms of speaking up for Miranda's sake, it was much easier for her to imagine having difficult conversations with her mother.

Many mothers in their thirties, forties, and fifties are comfortable talking about their feelings, but many of our own older mothers are (or were) not. Some may feel defensive when we broach the subject of our relationship, and a mere disagreement may be considered disrespectful. Luckily my own mother does not consider a disagreement between us disrespectful. However, it has still been very hard for her not to take my life choices personally as a rejection of her own choices. And when I am with her, I still find my behavior prone to being curiously erratic and angry—much the embarrassing opposite of my usual confidence as a fifty-five-year-old counselor and clinician.

I know that at these times, I am still essentially stuck in a very old complex or pattern: I am still seeking my mother's approval, for the umpteenth time, only to discover once again that she does not approve—much less find the pride that I girlishly want her to have—in my way of life. Faced with what to a child would feel like a catastrophic abandonment, I, too, drop back into an all-too-familiar despair, and so the cycle goes on. It is difficult for me to admit that these patterns, which I first was able to trace in my adolescence, persist now, more than forty years later, and that there are times when I still don't have control over my behavior when I am in the presence of my mother. My acting out may be less frequent, but it is still intense and painful. To this day of writing, I have been unable to fully accept what appears to be true: that for her own reasons, my mother is not actually interested in my world of ideas and experience. Here our matriline has assumed its strong tidal and generational pull and has proved stronger than we two can overcome so far. This impasse between us has left me to do the work myself—to consciously compensate for it, at some danger and with great effort, with my own self and daughter. As so often happens, my wound has become my life's work, my handhold to understanding the complexity of ordinary people's everyday lives. Indeed I share with lots of mothers what feels like a kind of matrilineal tragedy: that we—my mother and her daughter, both of whom have good intentions—just haven't been able to create a strong bond. Surely this needn't be so?

In my own case with my mother, there is a generational gap in communication styles in which the difference between talking about feelings that lurk below the surface—and emphatically *not* doing so—presents the different strategic choices for survival that most separate our two camps. In this generational disconnect with my mother, I sense that whenever we try to discuss any small conflicts that might be going on between us now, we each appear to be stuck in our own kind of post-traumatic stress reaction to our earlier skirmishes. Remarkably, however, in my midlife, I have found a way to heal some of the pain and blame I have projected onto my mother for not feeling accepted and loved for who *I* am. I have done so without the need to actually involve her in my own internal process. This has at least allowed me to raise my own daughter mostly free of these same clashes of language and values, and to write a book in which our voices are respected for what they are—voices that are different but in sync.

Indeed, this last step has been a miraculous lesson, a piece of magic I would never have considered possible back in my angry adolescent days. I have learned that for there to be healing, our mothers do not need to participate in a therapeutic process—ours or their own. For that matter, they do not need to be alive in order for us to heal. We can heal our emotional legacies in many ways. For example, we can learn to cultivate a positive "inner mother"—a way of being with ourselves that is highly attuned to and respectful of our own emotional needs. In essence, we can learn to mother ourselves, and in so doing, we can repair our wounds. If we find another who can mirror and contain us without judgment, that individual can also help us heal. Thomas Lewis, Fari Amini, and Richard Lannon, the three physicians and authors of the classic

A General Theory of Love, teach that love from another—a partner, a spouse, a friend, a therapist—can literally create new circuitry in our adult limbic brains and mend our adult nervous systems. *Love matters.* They write:

> If someone's relationships today bear a troubled imprint, they do
> so because an influential relationship left its mark on a child's
> mind. When a limbic connection has established a neural pattern,
> it takes a limbic connection to revise it.[3]

Lewis, Amini, and Lannon go on to say that if, for example, therapy works, it transforms a patient's brain and his emotional landscape forever. "Thus the urgent necessity for a therapist to get his emotional house in order."[4] And I say that the same is true of us mothers: there is an urgent necessity to get our emotional houses in order as we mother our adolescent daughters.

I want to be clear that I am not saying that therapy is the only way for us mothers to get our emotional houses in order, but it has been one of my ways. It was not a crisis that sent me into therapy. Instead, I felt compelled to start the process because, like Sally, I wanted to learn how to express feelings in ways that I hadn't learned from my parents, and I wanted to better understand the complexities of my relationship with my mother. Once I became a mother, the healing of my legacy felt more urgent. This is the healing in my own life that I have, in Marion Woodman's words, "been called on to incorporate." *Incorporate* means literally "bring into one's body" (*corporis* is Latin for "body"), and there is no doubt that in my healing, I have incorporated a capacity to regulate my emotional reactions. What I mean by this is that when I am working out a conflict with someone, I am able to detach, in healthy ways, and my nervous system doesn't get as rattled as it used to. I am able to be in relationship with family and friends in ways that I never could have imagined. This, however, does not mean I don't make mistakes. I make plenty of mistakes in all of my relationships, but I have learned to trust my intuition and to read my own and others' feelings with a high degree of accuracy. As a mother, these skills have served me well. I have had a similar calling in my professional life—that is, to assist mothers in healing their emotional and psychological legacies as they face the challenges of raising their adolescent daughters and as their daughters look to them for their true emotional inheritance, an inheritance that is unburdened by emotional baggage from their matrilineal line.

MY MATRILINEAL INHERITANCE

As a teenager (and later in my life, as well), when I would ask my mother about her relationship with her mother, she would give a very rational and reasonable response. Without any evident emotion, she would review my grandmother's life of infirmity and her early death at age forty-seven from heart failure, when my mother was just twenty-five years old. My grandmother was one of five sisters raised in upstate New York, and she had been chronically ill, more or less from birth, with severe asthma and allergies. Her condition was exacerbated by the cold weather, and so, at the age of eight, she was sent to live with a family friend in Virginia. This was 1917, when long-distance phone calls were reserved for special occasions and long-distance travel was expensive and time-consuming. Trips to visit a lonely daughter were most likely few and far between. How did my grandmother fare so far away from her parents at such a young age? Her physical health improved, yet I often wonder about her emotional health. What internal conflicts must she have felt? How did her parents help her deal with her inevitable homesickness? How openly was she able to talk to her parents and her substitute family in Virginia?

My mother was always very respectful when she talked about her own mother, a woman, of course, I had never known. My mother would describe how, upon arriving home from school every afternoon, she would be required to take a good scrubbing bath before entering the shaded bedroom where her mother was resting in bed. In my heart, I fast-forward to my mother's discomfort in being physically affectionate with me as a girl, and I wonder whether she, a single child, had ever been able to spontaneously cuddle with her mother. And my grandmother—what of her? How could she have cuddled with her own mother when that mother was hundreds of miles away?

My mother has never cared for my delving. Her opinion about exploring maternal legacy seems quite like her opinion about psychotherapy. "Why upset the apple cart?" she asks. I can respect her opinion. In fact, there have been many painful periods in my life when I have wished that I wasn't quite so devoted to upsetting the apple cart. But it has been my nature and my destiny to understand this legacy, and my drive to do so has, at times, made me feel as if my very survival were at stake.

As a delver, I felt very sad about my mother's account of her mother. Our conversations about my grandmother always ended with my mother's generous refrain: "She did the best she could." But perhaps in her unflagging respect for her mother, I sensed there was something missing in her own emotional affect. Even at a young age, it seemed to me that my mother was carrying an emotional wound, that she had somehow missed an emotional step in reaching her practical conclusion, as though she hadn't examined and assimilated her feelings. After all, coming from her generation, how could she have, and with whom? Although I came to respect her choice not to do any personal excavations of her own, I was never fully satisfied. Marion Woodman's words helped me understand my dissatisfaction:

> Parents were once children themselves, trapped in their parents' complexes. Often it was a parent's silent pain which was most excruciating to the sensitive child. No matter what [the child] did to make the parent happy, the sadness never went away. That sadness of the [parent's] soul becomes part of the child's inheritance.[5]

Even as a girl, although I certainly was not conscious of it, I felt compelled to finish a step for my mother and my grandmother. Indeed, it is what my psychological work would become—solving the puzzle of my grandmother's and mother's emotional legacy. And so I ask the same of you: How was your mother's relationship with her mother, or your grandmother's relationship with her mother? Perhaps your mother has emotional memories that would be important for you to know. If your mother has passed on or if you're not comfortable asking her about her relationship with her mother, can other family members shed light on your matrilineal inheritance? Are there feelings—your mother's or your own—that need to be acknowledged and expressed? I urge you to find an outlet for these feelings, because they may unconsciously find their way into the middle of how you communicate with your teenage daughter. Writing about them in a journal and reflecting on them is a good first step.

When Eliza was born, I couldn't believe that a girl was mine to keep! I have three brothers and no sisters, and I felt I was being given a second chance with my maternal legacy. The first ten years of raising Eliza were full of sleep-deprived connection and joy, and my love for her was easy to access. Cuddling with her came naturally to me, and I felt such confidence as a mother. Then, during her eleventh year, Eliza's stirrings began. At first, the intimations of a new restlessness were emerging. I remember how she would sometimes bolt out of the house, for no apparent reason, and take a brisk walk back and forth along our long driveway. I knew she was fine, and I was fundamentally pleased with her capacity to know what she needed: to be outside, moving her lanky body, walking, pondering her life, and developing her own inner life. She always returned refreshed but not wanting to chat. Chatting away with me had been a daily ritual. But now she had recently begun a habit of writing in a journal, and I temporarily lost my confidence as a mother. Even though I knew that she was discovering her own very healthy ways of becoming her own distinct, unique self, it triggered intense feelings of abandonment in me, because she was distancing herself from me. I began to actually panic.

Why? I'm certain it was because I had been that age when I had begun to move away from my own mother. Slowly but surely over the years that followed, my distancing turned into anger, confusion, and sadness, and these feelings gathered with great intensity until I rejected my mother almost completely. My mother did not know how to help me or how to reach me. By sixteen, I felt lost and depressed. I was at boarding school, eating to suppress my feelings, and without the help and guidance that I needed. Underneath the layers of anger, sadness, and fat, I longed for my mother.

This is the memory that I held on to for dear life when Eliza started to pull away. It was this memory that helped me know that when an adolescent daughter is pulling away and finding her own way, separate from her mother, she still needs her mother—not less than but perhaps even more than ever. Somehow I knew that the loneliness I had felt as a teenage daughter did not have to be repeated and that I could learn how to mother my teenage daughter well, stay connected to her, and be central to helping her navigate the ups and downs of adolescence. I suspected that if I could gather all of my inner and outer resources, our relationship could even thrive. But this stance required me to reject the cultural prejudice that teenage girls are impossible to manage and that they are unreasonable and unstable creatures. I could not accept this or the prevailing cultural belief that if mother and daughter can just *survive* the adolescent years, then they will be successful. I have witnessed how this assumption can freeze mothers in their tracks, with conventional wisdom having them believe that there is no point in even trying because their efforts would make no difference.

Worse still, I have seen how their memories of rocky adolescent relationships with their own mothers compound and reinforce this reality.

FORWARD AND BACKWARD ALONG THE MATRILINE

I had a college roommate whose parents were Holocaust survivors. Once, she and I were talking about the impact of trauma on the nervous systems of first- and second-generation immigrants. She, a first-generation immigrant, was remarking on her own inexplicable anxiety, her hypervigilance, and her tendency to always fear the worst. By contrast, she was fascinated by my relatively laid-back approach to life and my "cup half-full" view of the world. How could we two close friends—both having had relatively trauma-free childhoods, both children of responsible, loving (if undemonstrative) parents—be experiencing the world so differently?

At some point in our discussion, I thought about a young woman named Priscilla Mullins. She was a pilgrim who came across the Atlantic on the Mayflower in 1620, landing on the coast of our North American continent on a spot that would be named Plymouth. A girl of eighteen years, she was traveling with her deeply devout parents and her brother with the hope of a new beginning. But that very first winter, two-thirds of the passengers and crew of 150 would die of starvation and disease. Priscilla Mullins would be the only member of her family to survive. I am interested in how she must have felt that very spring when she married a fellow passenger named John Alden. She had left the life she had known in Europe to come to a harsh landscape of brutally hot summers and deathly cold winters. She'd just lost her mother, father, and brother, as well as most of the community with whom she had come to this new land. I can easily conjure the pain and the trauma that she withstood. And I marvel that she and John went on to have eleven children and to prosper and eventually pass away at their large farm in nearby Duxbury, surrounded by their thriving brood.

I brought her to mind in this discussion because Priscilla was my great-grandmother fourteen generations ago, after whom both my grandmother and I (and many others in my family) were named. My mother's first name is Alden. Most of us are immigrants in this country of ours, and all share in the legacy of perseverance and experimentation that the American story has become. Only half-joking, my friend and I agreed that perhaps I had a few hundred years more than she to work my forebears' relocation and trauma out of my nervous system. Her family's nightmare would need more time.

I remember one tense exchange that I had with my mother when I was around fifteen. I was giving her a piece of my mind—about what, I'm not sure. I'm guessing I was feeling angry and critical of what I felt was her incapacity to understand and love me, of her inability to "get me"—that oh-so-familiar adolescent refrain. In a moment of reflection, she told me about her mother's inability to mother her well, and she insisted that she was doing a better job than her mother had done. Remarkably, she was not being defensive. She really wanted me to understand what a miracle her mothering was—however imperfect—given her lack of mothering by a chronically ill mother. She told me that I would have the tools to do an even better job with my children.

Now I cherish this moment when she helped me to look forward along the matrilineal line and see progress. It makes me reflect back down the line, to one of Priscilla Alden's many daughters—the one named Elizabeth, from whom I am descended. How hard it must have been to share her tired mother with ten siblings. This thought leads me to consider, for the umpteenth time, how difficult it must have been for my mother to have a mother who was chronically ill and how grateful I am for everything that my mother *has been* able to give me. Now at this juncture, seeing Eliza out and about in the world's business, I can see that my mother, too, did the best that she could.

This is part of the healing in my own life that I have incorporated and that I am passing on to Eliza. It does not mean that I have been a perfect mother, and I know I have not been a perfect daughter. What it does mean is that our matriline is ever-evolving in the direction of greater love, under-standing, and acceptance, and for this, Eliza and I can be grateful.

3

A Mother's Intuition

The intuitive mind is a sacred gift, and the rational mind is a faithful servant.
We have created a society that honors the servant and has forgotten the gift.
—ALBERT EINSTEIN

ELIZA AND I HAVE FOUND that very few girls ever become too cool to listen to a good story. In our Mothering & Daughtering preteen workshops, we always read a Russian fairy tale that tells the story of a young girl faced with a series of tests who survives by the use of her inner "guide"—a doll that has been handmade for her by her mother. Like many fairy tales, *Vasilisa the Wise* is complete with a dark forest, a frightening witch, and a trio of antagonists who wish an innocent girl harm. And like all fairy tales, what is an apparently straightforward story actually offers us a world rich in meaning and metaphor.

In discussing the story in our workshops with both mothers and daughters, it quickly becomes clear that this is a tale about a girl learning to know and trust her intuitive voice. With the help of her doll, Vasilisa is guided into the dark woods to ask for fire from the fearsome Baba Yaga. Once she has arrived at Baba Yaga's hovel, Vasilisa must accomplish impossible tasks to earn that fire and it is only with the help of her doll—her inner intuitive voice—that she finds solutions. If, during adolescence, we miss the gift of learning to know our intuitive voice so that we might be guided through whatever "dark woods" we come upon, then it's almost inevitable that we will be called upon to walk that difficult path later in life (as I was). Any circumstance that challenges us emotionally—divorce, recovery from an addiction, a loss of any kind, even parenting an adolescent—can be a catalyst for completing our adolescent maturation process, so that we can learn to know and to trust our intuition and emotional intelligence.

Like our daughters, we mothers can always use a good story. Please turn to page 18 of the Daughtering side and read a condensed version of the Vasilisa tale written by Eliza. It's a perfect starting point for our discussion on intuition—a mother's best friend.

WHO *WAS* VASILISA'S MOTHER?

At the beginning of the story, Vasilisa's mother is on her deathbed, and we can only imagine the pain that she feels in knowing that she will not be alive to guide her daughter into womanhood. But let's turn from her death for a moment and put our attention on what else is dying in this tale. Since fairy tales mostly speak symbolically, it could be said that Vasilisa's relationship with her mother, as both of them have known it up to this point, is "dying." And so this story becomes a strong tale about individuation—the lifelong process of discovering one's true and independent self, a process that is just beginning for Vasilisa. This is where our daughters find themselves in this journey of adolescence—and they, like Vasilisa, are in search of their own intuitive wisdom and their own identity, separate from and yet still very connected to us.

Vasilisa and her troubles are the subject of Eliza's very first chapter. You can clearly see the message she is conveying to your daughter: intuition, or inner knowing—that is, knowing what's right for *you,* and not for your friends, teachers, advisers, or romantic partners—can be the very best guide out there in the real world, beyond the driveway. In a world that offers our children too many dangerous choices, you will rest much easier if you have confidence that your daughter has learned how to listen to and trust her own intuition. Helping her to do so is a gift of great value that will serve you both.

Therefore, let's be clear about something here: unlike Vasilisa's mother, we are alive to assist our daughters! Luckily, your teen won't have to make her way through the woods with nothing more than the help of her inner voice. No matter where she is, it's likely that you are just a text message away. You can (and should) be there to give her reality checks as she navigates the shoals of teen life. Giving your daughter a reality check about her intuitive sense of things can sound something like this: "You really have a good reading on this situation." Or "Your intuition about people is right on." Or "I think you can really trust your gut here given all that you have told me." Of course, we say these things only when we believe them or see evidence of their truth. The point is that we can and should look for opportunities to do so.

What about when your daughter makes a poor choice and gets herself in a fix? Timed right and approached sensitively, you can help her review what led up to her poor choice. I tried hard whenever I could to keep my judgments at bay when I approached Eliza about poor choices. She was already feeling bad enough about having made a poor choice. By helping her review what had led up to her choice, I could almost always help her locate the moment when she "heard" but did not follow her intuition. We mothers have certainly discovered over time that it is in the aftermath of our own mistakes that we learned the most about our intuition. We have honed our intuition by learning from our mistakes, and we can pass on the wisdom of our experiences to our daughters; they do not have to learn everything from scratch! Like Vasilisa's mother, we can give our daughters the gift of the doll that *we* have made for *them*. The doll is made in Vasilisa's likeness for a reason: the doll is mirroring back the accuracy of Vasilisa's intuitive perceptions and giving her confidence in her emotional intelligence so that she might have better and better access to her inner knowing throughout her life.

Although the story holds obvious wisdom for our daughters, it holds an equally valuable, though slightly less obvious, wisdom for us mothers. From our vantage point, *Vasilisa the Wise* is a tale about the sense of urgency that once existed but that now may feel irrelevant to us modern and rootless folk: a woman's intuition is passed from mother to daughter, one generation to the next. Vasilisa's gift from her mother—the doll, which Vasilisa pays close attention to—is what saves her from losing her way in the dark. The doll performs impossible tasks in her service, and once the tasks are accomplished, it guides Vasilisa back home. And like any heroine, Vasilisa must meet and slay her "dragon" before she returns home. I think the dragon that Vasilisa successfully "slays" is her *fear* of confronting the very fearsome Baba Yaga at her very scary hut in the deep, dark woods. In this story, Vasilisa's initiation is the "gift" from this hard-driving, but ultimately fair-playing, taskmistress. (To therapists like me, Baba Yaga is the unsung, falsely maligned heroine of the story, as witches often are!) Vasilisa returns home triumphant, her creative fire in hand, initiated into womanhood by the challenges she has met and overcome. Psychologically speaking, she has integrated the gift of her mother's intuition (and some of the power of Baba Yaga's wisdom) and made it her own.

Intuition, of course, cannot literally be passed from one person to another. Rather, it is something that each of us must learn to cultivate on our own. Thus, it is an essential detail in the story that Vasilisa's mother gives her daughter a doll in Vasilisa's own likeness, making sure that her daughter will be able to cultivate her *own* intuition. But as our daughters learn to cultivate their intuition, they need us to be there to help them. They need to witness us responding to our own intuitive voice, and they need our input and encouragement along the way as their inner doll comes to life. And without guidance from their inner voice and from us, they *will* get lost along the way as they explore complex issues regarding, among other things, friendship and intimacy, sexuality and safety, and the balance of work and play. It is so fitting that Vasilisa's doll accomplishes seemingly impossible tasks, as our daughters must also learn that they can find solutions to seemingly impossible situations, with our help and the help of their inner guidance system—their intuition. But what is intuition, really?

INTUITION BASICS

I have learned that the answer to the question "What is intuition?" is found in both fairy tales and neuroscience. It has been by dipping into both of these deep wells that I have come to define *intuition* as an internal perception, not arrived at through thought, which facilitates insight and understanding. It is through an internal "seeing" and an internal "hearing" that we come to an internal, or inner, "knowing." This is a kind of knowing that is different from what we customarily rely on in our culture. Intuitive wisdom can appear irrational; it can lead us to what seem like crazy choices about love and work and other large questions that won't stay within the narrower frame of reference that logic and facts require. Therefore, intuition is frequently judged negatively in our culture, which is very much in love with rational intelligence and externally definable goals. In the face of this undertow of concrete linear thinking (which, don't get me wrong, is essential to our survival), it helps to realize that intuition is, in fact, another form of intelligence. (See Daughtering, pages 56–65, where Eliza discusses emotional intelligence as it relates to all of us.)

Neuroscientist and medical intuitive Mona Lisa Schulz described the actual experience of intuition in this way:

Intuitive hits are sudden, immediate, and unexpected ideas. They seem illogical and have no clear line of thought. They frequently come out of the blue. Nevertheless, they bring with them a feeling of confidence and a certainty of their absolute indisputability.[1]

If we mothers can learn to listen for our intuition and to not judge or dismiss it when it comes to us in everyday life, it can help bring us more clarity and more confidence as we raise our daughters. We have all heard stories about "mother's intuition." Some of us have had the absolute certainty, like a bolt coming out of the blue, of knowing that our child is in danger or needs help, even at a distance or despite apparent evidence to the contrary. In fact, some mothers have saved their children's lives by trusting their gut in unforeseen traumatic situations, where knowledge and rational thinking are unavailable or actually misleading. Dr. Schulz calls this kind of insight *clairsentience,* or the ability to feel another person's physical state in one's own body. She also suggests that there is an evolutionary basis in the need for a mother to have an intuitive sense of what her baby needs, especially when it is in pain. Many mothers of infants, for instance, describe the experience of waking up in the middle of the night a minute or two before their baby starts crying. It's as if their nervous system has said, "You're on call, and you're about to be summoned by a hungry/wet/feverish child. Might as well get ready."

This sensing of what your child needs when she is a baby need not end when she is sleeping through the night or toddling off into the larger world. It need not end when she begins school or starts riding a bicycle. And it especially need not end when she approaches the teenage years and spends more time with her peers. Knowing what your child needs, whatever her age, doesn't necessarily refer to what she needs in a dramatic situation or in one involving danger. It could be as mundane as knowing when to help her with her homework or knowing when she needs time alone.

As I have honed my mother's intuition over the past couple of decades, I have learned to "read" it in my body. It is in one's body where intuition becomes concrete and perceptible—or what I have come to call *embodied.* It is through our senses that intuition's messages come through: feeling our heart beat a little faster, our in-breath becoming more shallow, "chills" running up the back of our spine, or having an a-ha moment as our face flushes.

But what is the difference between intuition and unwarranted fear? Certainly we have experienced many of these bodily symptoms when we are afraid. How do we know when our reflexive "No!" has nothing to do with our daughter and everything to do with a memory of some trouble *we* got into as a teenager? Or some story we heard on the news? A reactive "No!" is often a clue that there is unwarranted fear. Intuition brings with it a certainty that is felt in the body and the mind—even when we are afraid, intuition has a calming effect—because we *know* we have made the right decision. Our "No" does not need the exclamation point, because it has gravitas—that is, it is grounded in our intuition and based on our experience of our daughter in the present. Even though our own teenage experience might inform our decision and we may feel real fear about the request, if our decision really comes from our inner knowing, our "No" is likely to be nonreactive and will ground us. *Intuition is a very reliable tool because, unlike theories and advice, it can always be applied to the unique situation at hand.* And what better tool is there for us to "give" our daughter for her life's journey?

Vasilisa's mother gives her daughter the guiding function of intuition so that her daughter can stay true to herself, even when her mother is no longer there to perceive her needs. Assuming that we mothers received the gift of our "doll"—whether from our own mother or our father, a mentor, or life's lessons—we have the good fortune of being able to use that guiding function as we mother our daughters. We might use it, for instance, to help us know how and when to talk with her about the disparaging comments she has been making about her changing body, or how and when to talk with her about why we are concerned about her hanging out with a certain group of friends.

An embodied Vasilisa feels her intuition "speaking" to her through the sensation of the doll jumping up and down in her pocket. *Embodied* means that one is truly inhabiting one's body and listening to one's bodily cues. When Vasilisa pays attention to her doll, it protects her. The doll's demonstrations remind me vividly of the "butterflies" some of us get in our stomach when our intuitive wisdom is "talking" to us. If we really listen to what our body is telling us, then we know that our daughter will *not* be going out to that party—even though she says everyone else will be there—and we will know how to stand firm as she protests our decision. To continue to hone your intuition, turn to page 28 of Daughtering for Eliza's "Intuition Guidelines."

BRAIN BASICS

Biologically speaking, we have two essentially separate brains—the right brain and the left brain. They are connected by a "bridge" called the *corpus callosum*. This evolutionarily extravagant setup allows each brain to process the same information in a different way and then to share and integrate the information via the bridge. Although both the right and left brains can perform each other's functions, the left hemisphere is predominantly logical, linear, efficient, and fact-based in its perception of the world. Its incredibly practical strengths include rational analysis, the creation of structure, and an affinity for math and science. It is often popularly called the "masculine" side of the brain.

The right hemisphere of the brain, popularly called the "feminine" side, is more tuned into emotions, more widely receptive, more visual, and more contextual than the left hemisphere. Its natural strengths involve emotional intelligence, reading the body's signals, and seeing the whole picture and the relational aspects of that picture, rather than simply its separate parts in isolation. When using words such as *feminine* and *masculine* to describe the different sides of the brain, it is important to remember that all men and women have both masculine and feminine sides of the brain. A man can have a very developed, and even dominant, right, or feminine, brain—just as a woman can have a very developed, and even dominant, left, or masculine, brain. Like the two halves of the yin/yang symbol, the masculine and feminine brains are complementary. Neither is complete unto itself, and both are necessary to make a whole.

That being said, neuroscience has now established that the right hemisphere of the brain has developed a deeper connection with the physical body than the left hemisphere, and that women have significantly more neurological pathways between the right hemisphere of their brains and the rest of their bodies than do men.[2] It follows that most women are slightly better wired than men to be in touch with their brain-body information highways. It's not surprising, then, that we women are more likely to talk about intuitive messages that we receive from our bodies. It is relatively common to hear women talk about "trusting their gut" or "following their heart" or "feeling it in their bones," even though our left-brain-dominated culture often pooh-poohs such statements as nonsense. But it is time for our attitudes to catch up with brain science!

When Eliza and I take out our workshop easel to make two lists of what C. G. Jung called the masculine and feminine *principles*—that is, qualities or attributes in the psyches of both men and women that can correlate to the different functions of the left and right hemispheres of the brain—the adolescent daughters at the workshop can easily compile the lists of opposites. They absolutely know about the split between these opposing principles: logic *versus* intuition, doing *as opposed to* being, goal *instead of* process, thinking *over* feeling, assertiveness *in lieu of* empathy, linear *rather than* contextual, rational *versus* relational, action *over* patience, ambition *instead of* generosity, and on and on. Sadly, the daughters can just as easily identify which list of attributes is undervalued in our culture. They know that their capacity to be intuitive (they call it *trusting your gut),* emotional, and empathetic is often viewed as weak or inferior when compared with their capacity for accessing the rational and goal-oriented parts of their left brain. In our weekend-workshop community, we make a point of paying more attention to these undervalued and overlooked gifts of the feminine principle, and we urge the mothers and daughters to work from these places as a group. In a few short hours and days, we find that cultivating these gifts can lead to better communication, more confidence, and, quite literally, peace of mind.

Did you, too, forget the gift of intuition that Einstein refers to in the quote at the start of this chapter? I did. For me, this gift went underground during adolescence, due in part to the intellectual battle fatigue I experienced in school. I think that an unacknowledged part of me—okay, let's say it anatomically: an entire one of my two brains—gave up, because it felt overwhelmed by my teachers' emphasis on rational processes. The emotional intelligence I possessed (like most children do possess, in great, untempered quantities) was simply not appreciated or developed in any of the schools that I attended, nor was it encouraged by my parents. (To be fair, it had not been seen or encouraged by their parents, either.) I am certain that my adolescence would have been much less challenging if I had learned to recognize and value my intuitive wisdom and understand how it could work with my rational mind more fruitfully.

Luckily, this intuitive part of me came dramatically to life in midcareer, inspired by the writings and mentorship of Jungian author and analyst Marion Woodman. Her influential work over the past forty years has been devoted to helping women find value in the intuitive and relational "feminine" side of their being. By reading and training in her work, I began to feed and take care of "my doll," and my doll started to respond. What I noticed as I cultivated my intuition and other right-brain attributes was that I felt more and more content—at home in my body, at peace in my relationships, and more devoted to and inspired by my work. My nervous system, no doubt, was responding to a more balanced use of my brain, and it calmed down. This balanced state is a natural state for us human beings if we learn to get out of our own way—out from under the domination of the left hemisphere of the brain. Jung described the work of maturing and balancing the masculine and feminine principles of the psyche as an important part of the process of individuation, something he considered a lifelong endeavor. When our left and right hemispheres are balanced, we are able to experience a kind of homeostasis of the psyche. Having learned about homeostasis of the body in biology class, I was fascinated by the idea that the brain is also "wired" to seek this same internal balance.

The left brain's idea of wholeness can get confused with the idea of perfection—a goal that is unattainable in this world. When the left brain is dominant, Woodman warns, we can become addicted to perfection. No doubt, this is of grave concern to watchful mothers as we raise our daughters in a culture that guides them to believe that they can achieve the unachievable: perfect bodies, perfect grades, and perfect happiness.

The new brain science is helping us understand that both brain hemispheres are wired to work together and that both are involved in feeling *and* thinking. However, the two hemispheres are coming from very different perspectives. Almost a century ago, Jung presaged this psychological reality and called it the *inner marriage.* He said that if we are to achieve wholeness, we must have a balanced working relationship between the masculine and feminine parts of our psyche. As we achieve this balance, we will feel less stress and conflict in our lives.

In my experience with mothering, by following these greats I have learned that we need perspective from both parts of our brain. It is best if we learn to allow the right brain—the "gift" of intuition—to lead the way and to let the left brain be the servant to this gift. Isn't it extraordinary that this most current and cutting-edge science supports ancient wisdom from a long, long time ago that has been buried inside our "simple" Russian fairy tale? Buried, indeed, but *alive!*

GIVING YOURSELF A DOLL FIRST

It can be useful for us to hold a view of Vasilisa's mother in the context of the *motherline*—that is, from the point of view of the many generations of women who have come before her. We have already spoken about the matriline and maternal inheritance in chapter 2. Now, let's look at it in terms of our fairy tale. Vasilisa's mother could give a doll to Vasilisa because *she, too, had been given a doll by her mother.* We can assume that the same was true with Vasilisa's grandmother and great-grandmother and great-great-grandmother, and so on along the matriline. In this fairy tale at least, it is easy to imagine this blessing going unbroken for many, many generations.

But this is not so in our culture. A principle challenge in our time—huge in its latent impact—is that many of us mothers never received "a doll" from our mothers, nor did our mothers receive one from their mothers, and so on. A woman's grasp of her intuitive wisdom may be weak as a result of it not being passed on consciously and deliberately by her mother, but when she "discovers" it in other ways, as I did in my midlife, it can reemerge, blossom, and be fully utilized.

There are many ways to be initiated into becoming a wise, intuitive woman, and all of them likely involve some willingness on our part to experience our own pain, self-doubt, loneliness, and uncertainty. Reading that list of feelings, one can see why adolescence is a time of initiation: all of these challenging feelings are usually present in spades during the teen years. But just feeling them is not enough. One reason my adolescent maturation process was incomplete was that I was an almost entirely peer-oriented teenager, and peers simply cannot supply enough wise, emotional support to allow difficult emotions to be expressed, understood, and integrated. My peers did not have the capacity to provide the mirroring and containing (which I discuss in chapters 4 and 5) that I needed. My unexpressed feelings went underground, as yours may have. And as I watched my adolescent daughter process the inevitable pain of growing into an independent person, my incomplete adolescent feelings made their way back up to my consciousness—just as yours may be doing now.

My emotional initiation came in midlife, when I was strong enough to face these painful feelings head-on and get the support I needed to "complete" my adolescence. It was as though a developmental piece had not been finished, and I needed to find a way to process emotions I had never learned to name or feel. If I hadn't been willing to face my pain, I believe that my life would have suffered a kind of flattening out instead of the expansion that occurred. I learned that it was in passing through the experience of feeling what I feared to feel (a deep existential sadness and loneliness) that a deep initiation took place, and I came to know my own intuition.

If you are looking at this same fear and if the price seems high, consider the gift that awaits you: a survivor's grounding in the wisdom of intuition, an innate intelligence that knows what is good for you, knows what you need next, and knows it with lightning speed. And of crucial importance, it knows how to pass these gifts on to your daughter.

INTUITION AND YOUR FEMININE BODY

It goes without saying that as our daughter's body becomes a woman's body, she will look to us for guidance more and more. The more practiced we are in living comfortably in our feminine body and its cycles, the more likely it is that our daughter will inherit this same ease. Studies have shown that women have greater access to their intuition during the premenstrual phase of their cycle.[3] It is possible, therefore, that we can look at our menstrual cycle as part of our inner-guidance system, and we can teach our daughters to do so as well, guiding them to understand, among other things, that there may be optimal times in their cycles to be creative and productive, to rest and reflect, and to honor deep feelings. When we are attuned to our natural rhythms and when we listen to our body's needs, our intuitive voice is not shut out and instead has room to speak.

In her beautifully insightful book *Eating in the Light of the Moon,* psychologist Dr. Anita Johnston suggests that we should think of PMS as referring to "premenstrual sensitivity" rather than the diagnosis of "premenstrual syndrome." Dr. Johnston refers to emotional sensitivity, which comes from the realm of the heart and is an attribute of the right "feminine" hemisphere of the brain. I don't need to remind you that this is the kind of sensitivity that is dismissed in our culture. Many of us have heard, all our lives, the all-too-popular refrain, "You're being too sensitive!" Emotional sensitivity can be judged to the point of being pathologized, and many of us learn to apologize for our sensitivity, premenstrual or not, rather than to honor it. But it's this very sensitivity that can send us important messages.

I know that PMS symptoms, such as mood changes, water retention, food cravings, and headaches, are real (I have experienced them, too), and that they can even be debilitating. But I found that when I began to appreciate that the symptoms I was having premenstrually might have meaning beyond the physical and emotional discomfort they caused, I began to feel better. When I listened to my body's premenstrual messages—my emotional sensitivities, my hungers (sometimes including emotional eating), and even my dreams—my relationship to my body and my emotions changed. It became clear to me that my emotional sensitivity was often triggered by things that needed to be brought to consciousness. Eventually, my premenstrual sensitivity began to feel like a gift of insight, rather than a curse. Truly welcoming and appreciating my menstrual cycles also helped make my transition into menopause much easier.

Our bodies are the tuning forks for reading our intuition; they are the instruments through which many of our intuitive messages come to us. If we tune out our premenstrual emotional and physical messages, we may miss important information. For example, we might miss information that would help us become more nutritionally balanced. Eliza has watched me eat well and care for my body with supplements, rest, and exercise. She has learned to watch her own menstrual cycle, because she, like me, is premenstrually sensitive. She does not experience her symptoms as a curse, though. She has learned to listen to her body and to slow down and rest, as needed, before her period. She enjoys this relationship that she has with her body, and she appreciates feeling in sync with, instead of dominated by, her cyclical sensitivity. I am not sure that she would have resolved this for herself at such a young age had she not seen me take care of myself in such a way.

Be aware of inner critical voices you may have about your body shape and size. These voices can be like radio static when you're trying to listen to the intuitive wisdom coming through your body. If you are at war with your body, it will be hard to listen well. Body acceptance functions like a cease-fire, and it can help create peace of mind. This peace of mind can help you cultivate a capacity to listen to your body's messages: intuitive messages that guide you, hunger cues that keep you at your body's natural weight, symptoms of stress that can tell you to slow down, sexual desire that leads to more satisfying lovemaking, and menstrual and menopausal symptoms that can help you recognize and respect your natural, biological rhythms.

As we make peace with our body—our "soft animal body," as the poet Mary Oliver calls it—so too will our daughters follow suit. No matter what images the culture throws at her, you are still your daughter's greatest influence for body acceptance. By following your lead, she will accept and love her soft animal body, she will take good care of it, and it will purr. She will be in sync with its power and its many meaningful messages.

As we consider the Vasilisa tale and learn from its timeless lessons, perhaps we mothers can add another blessing for our time. Just as there is a blessing in a mother giving her daughter a doll—a reliable sense of the truth of her daughter's own intuition—there is a blessing in a mother giving her daughter a reliable sense of her strong, cyclical, and uniquely beautiful feminine body. And it is our mother's intuition that will show us when and how to bestow these blessings.

4

Mirroring a Soul

It's [a mother's] task to create a space in which [her] child can grow into its own being—be who it was born to be. In other words, she will mirror the child to itself.
—MARION WOODMAN

"SHE JUST DOESN'T GET ME, and she never will!" fifteen-year-old Molly wails during a break at a recent thirteen- to fifteen-year-old Mothering & Daughtering workshop.

Our group of twenty-five mothers and twenty-five daughters has been doing paired communication exercises, and the moms and daughters are stretching and taking a break. As we often do, Eliza and I have stepped outside our large meeting space in order to mediate—this time after one of the exercises between Molly and her mother, Claire, has turned into an argument. Molly is glaring at us through her tears, and Claire looks beat. Eliza and I quickly decide to split up the embattled pair for a few minutes. I take Molly aside, while Eliza focuses on reviving Claire.

Molly doesn't look at me as I ask her ever so gently what's going on. Even though the specific topic of her argument with her mother had been Molly's curfew time, it doesn't surprise me that in her upset state, Molly's first words actually get to the heart of things: "She just doesn't get me, and she never will!" A teenage daughter can be like an oracle that sees only in black and white, with her wisdom coming from an uncensored and eloquent place. Molly was giving me one clear message, a message that she repeated for her mom in no uncertain terms when I brought them back together: "I need to be seen and heard!"

Do you remember how you felt when you were a teenage daughter trying to get through to your mother? Thinking back on those years, even if only for a minute, may help you feel some compassion for your daughter during heated exchanges like Molly and Claire's. Like all human beings, our daughters long to be seen and heard at the deepest level. Adolescents tend to feel this longing more intensely because they feel *everything* more intensely. Their brains are growing at the same tremendous rate as their bodies, and their hormones are, well, raging. And in the midst of all these physiological changes, they are also in the business of trying to become themselves, often under great scrutiny. In spite of what they may say, they need a lot of help from us right now.

For your daughter, a good part of that help will come in the form of your *mirroring* her thoughts and feelings. Attuning your responses to her ups and downs is quite literally like reflecting her in a mirror of her truest self—her soul. Mirroring your daughter is seeing her for who she is and reflecting back to her who you see, without judgment or agenda. The reflection can take the form of words, eyes connecting, facial expressions, physical gestures, or tone of voice. Mirroring your daughter doesn't necessarily mean that you repeat her words or gestures back to her. It means that what you do or say to your daughter (or anyone) communicates, "I see you, and I deeply value who you are and who you are becoming."

When Eliza and I came back together with Claire and Molly, we urged Claire to *really listen* to what Molly was saying about not being "gotten," instead of diving back into the problem of the curfew. We wanted Claire to remember that the root of the conflict was not so much about the curfew as it was about the act of listening and responding to (mirroring) Molly's constantly emerging self. Given the kaleidoscopic and tempestuous reality of teenagers, no doubt this is a Zen master's job. Yet again, we must dig down deep, muster our patience and forbearance, and let our daughters *daughter* us. We must let them show and tell us where they are (that day!), and then we must acknowledge, perhaps through something as simple as a smile or a nod, that we have truly heard and seen them. And next, lest we miss the forest (real living relationship) for the trees (conflicts about curfews and the like), we need to hear the best and deepest idea in the room—and that idea just might be coming from our daughter. Molly, in all of her daughtering wisdom, was desperately asking for Claire to see the forest. We mothers can miss this opportunity if we don't listen carefully. We need to really connect with our daughters before we talk about curfews or online limits or anything else.

But how do we see the forest? That day at the workshop, Eliza and I were not saying that the curfew issue didn't need to be worked out—there are lots of important conversations about limits and safety and responsibilities that need to be resolved with our kids. But we mothers must pause and take a breath before we get too focused on any one particular issue at hand. Only then might we find the mirroring capacity within ourselves that we can bring to every conversation that we have with our teenage daughters. This mirroring capacity is undeveloped in them and they will have a limited capacity to "get" where we are coming from. If you can remember that your job is to "get" your daughter and to "get" where she is coming from, she will feel seen and heard at her core. This does not mean that you need to agree with her or bend to her will—not at all. The trick is to not get distracted by the tree that is the topic at hand, so that the forest—your relationship with your daughter—will be in full view. If you learn to mirror your daughter's feelings in the midst of your conversations—for example, "I know how much you want to have a later curfew, because a lot of your friends have a later curfew than you"—and if you mean what you say, you will figure out a solution to the curfew issue and every other issue, together. And both mother and daughter will be the better for it.

The communication exercises in our preteen workshops are a piece of cake compared with the ones at the thirteen- to fifteen-year-old workshops, because the issues that need to be resolved rarely have to do with safety, drugs, alcohol, and boys. And yet even when they are younger, there is so much we can learn from our daughters by listening deeply to their emerging selves. I had an illuminating conversation during another break with Beatrice, a mother in one of our preteen workshops. In this particular session, we had done an exercise in which the girls had prepared a communication with Eliza's help—something they wanted to say to their mother that they really needed her to "get." Ten-year-old Ella, apparently for the umpteenth time, told Beatrice how very embarrassing it was for her when Beatrice sang and moved to music while driving the car, especially when it was in front of Ella's friends. What was illuminating for Beatrice—and illuminating for me as I listened—was that despite the many, many times that Ella had shared her embarrassment with her, Beatrice realized that she had never actually *heard* Ella. She confessed to me that she had laughed off Ella's feedback multiple times; she hadn't taken her daughter's feelings seriously because it hadn't been a serious matter to *her.*

To pause and to seriously consider what is important to our daughters, even if it's not important to us—in fact, especially if it's not important to us—emboldens them. I am not suggesting that our daughters dictate what our behavior should or shouldn't be; it's actually pretty hard for Eliza to move me off my point of view on lots of things. What I am suggesting is that we really hear what's going on with them, no matter how small or insignificant it seems. I am also not suggesting that we process with them for hours every time they have anything to say. Mirroring another soul, including the sometimes-entangled soul of our own daughters, is not necessarily a function of time. Beatrice's epiphany happened over the course of a few minutes. Afterward, she and Ella immediately broke through to a new place, and I could see Ella herself dancing around the room with delight. (Like mother, like daughter!) In the time it took to do a simple exercise, Beatrice realized what an impact listening to Ella at a deeper level could have on their relationship. Beatrice also realized (as I probably would have in her place) that she would likely still be singing and moving to the music when she drove the car most days—she didn't think she could change too much of who she fundamentally is. But she was ready to listen better and wake up to the fact that her ten-year-old girl was already beginning to carve out an identity for herself, and part of this carving involved struggling with what parts of her mother she might want to "reject" as she found that new and independent identity. From this experience, Beatrice was inspired to get into the habit of listening to Ella with more attunement. In other words, Beatrice came to see that Ella's issue about her singing was the *tree,* and her deeply listening to Ella (not blowing her off) was the *forest.*

For the sake of sanity, it may be important to state the obvious: the way our daughter *daughters* us can be insightful and visionary, but it can also be way off base. Eliza's frequent requests for time with her friends, both after school and on weekends, taught me to mirror her enthusiasm for her friendships while still holding the line in terms of her schedule staying sane. We mothers can mirror and still disappoint. Mirroring does not mean bowing to your daughter's wishes or agreeing with her all the time. Your adolescent daughter has wisdom, but not the wisdom of your years. In addition, she is still developing the frontal lobe of her brain, which will eventually give her the adult decision-making and reasoning processes that help inhibit impulsive behavior. Until then, we mothers can contribute the so-called *executive function* of our own frontal lobes to help teach our daughters to make the safest decisions when it comes to the Internet, curfews, boys, and parties.

Our mothering can be responsive, respectful, and attuned, but it will never be perfectly so. Undoubtedly, we will lose our perspectives and our tempers from time to time just as completely as our daughters do. However, it can be reassuring to know that if you don't "get" what your daughter is saying in the first round of a dispute, you can come back and repair any rupture with respect and attunement. (See page 109 for Eliza's discussion of "rupture and repair.") You can develop your mirroring skills and get better and better at seeing that in any conversation with your daughter, the priority needs to be the view of the forest—*really* hearing what she has to say and then guiding her on her journey of becoming herself.

MIRRORING BASICS

My definition of mothering—*raising your daughter to become herself*—was born out of my apprenticeship in soul making with Marion Woodman. I am sure her words at the start of this chapter are about *soul* when she speaks about a mother creating "a space in which [her] child can grow into its own being." As you most likely do, I take it as a given that we all have a unique character or essence that thrives when it is seen and valued. Child psychiatrist Donald Winnicott called this unique essence the *True Self.* When I use the word *soul,* I am referring to this True Self, and I am certain this is the place at our very core where we all long to be seen and heard. When soul is mirrored, we human beings thrive.

We mothers are the first mirror that our newborns gaze into. From the moment they open their eyes to their new world, babies are looking for the human face. Show them a simple drawing of the human face, and they will always prefer this image to others. What are they looking for? Why are they naturally drawn to the human face? Like the rooting reflex that helps them find a nipple, their neural programming leads them to a face. Just as a baby's physical survival depends on finding a nipple, her emotional survival depends on finding a human face, gazing into it at length, and having her own gestures and longings reflected back fluidly and safely. Just as a breast or bottle must have milk in it for a baby to thrive physically, the adult human face must be gazing back with an attuned response for the baby to thrive emotionally. That first face needs to be right there, returning a smile with a smile, a coo with a coo, a gesture of distress with an expression of concern.

Recently, scientists have identified and named *mirror neurons* in the brain. It is hypothesized that these neurons function to help us understand another's intention, speech, and actions. In your interactions with your adolescent daughter, this part of your brain works to help you understand her intentions so that you can respond to her (mirror her) with attunement. Mirror neurons probably help us read body language as well.

It is thought that mirror neurons make it possible for us to be attuned to our baby—and to our adolescent daughter—so we can feel empathy for her and thus provide care that is *contingent* with her emotional and physical needs. A contingent response is one that is just right; it's a response that *fits* the emotional need. It is the attuned response of the caregiver who "gets" the emotional need and responds effectively and in a timely manner.

Other kinds of adult responses—that is, ones that address more obvious, physical needs—are just as important in helping to create a baby's sense of safety and self. When we change a diaper when it needs changing, when we feed our daughter when she is hungry, when we wrap her in a blanket when she is cold, and when we rock her to sleep when she is tired, our baby girl thrives as a result of our care. She also begins to trust us and, by extension through us, to trust her universe. Research has shown that a baby's mirror neurons literally light up—are charged—by contingent emotional responses from her caregiver. It follows that as she feels our empathy, she slowly but surely develops the capacity to feel it for herself and for others. In other words, if we have responded to her without drama and with a gentle concern when she falls and scrapes her knee (instead of telling her she is fine and can stop crying now), she learns empathy and emotional intelligence. When we mirror her emotional and physical pain, she will learn to take care of herself when she is in pain and to recognize when another is in pain and in need of help. If we show up with consistency and appropriate emotional and physical responses to her needs as she moves through toddlerhood and childhood, she becomes an emotionally secure child. Children are emotionally secure not only because we have given them consistent and loving support, but also because we have taught them that all emotions are acceptable. We have mirrored back to them that it is okay—that it is natural and healthy—to feel sad and angry and frustrated and that it is a wonderful thing to feel the full range of human emotions.

Okay, let's fast-forward. How do we show up with consistency for our sometimes-surly and often emotionally inconsistent teenage daughter? For one thing, we need to be aware that mirroring an adolescent is less simple and less literal than mirroring an infant or child. With our teenage daughter, we need a more nuanced and flexible approach, and sometimes an *indirect* mirroring of her is more effective. Let's say your daughter arrives home after school on a day when she's been extremely anxious about communicating to her friend Sally about a misunderstanding they've had. Instead of saying, "How'd it go with Sally today?" you might say, "Hey there, want some tea?" Tone is important in any communication, but in indirect mirroring, it is everything. An empathetic invitation for tea together is really saying, "I am here. I want to listen. Come sit down with me." Even if your daughter doesn't want to talk about what happened with Sally, there's a reasonable chance that she will understand, on some level, what you are asking her, and your simple question will comfort her. (Don't necessarily expect her to show it, though.) She wants to be gotten, and you are showing and telling her that you want to get her.

There is no hard-and-fast rule here. Every teenage daughter is different, and each can be different from one day to the next and from one situation to the next. One afternoon it might be effective to ask her directly how it went with Sally, whereas another day it might be more effective to ask indirectly. You most likely already know that getting your adolescent kids to talk to you is more like horse whispering than anything else. This is why using your honed intuition is so important when mirroring your daughter. Your reading of the situation moment to moment will help you "find" her and "get" her. Your honed intuition, combined with your skill at mirroring, is an essential step in the always-improvisational mothering-as-a-martial-art dance. Imagine this mirroring "dance" between Eliza and me—an exchange we had when she returned home from school one day:

Sil: Hey, Sweetie, how're you doing?
Eliza: *Terrible.*
Sil: Oh, I'm so sorry to hear that. Want to tell me about what's going on?
Eliza: No. Not now.
Sil: Okay. Just know that I am right here if you want to talk.

Now this was the kind of exchange in which I had to really contain myself and not say another word! This exchange is an example of basic mirroring; yet, even basic mirroring is not so simple. Even though you can read the words on this page, you can't watch and feel the many nuances of tone and body language that are the other dimensions of such an exchange. But trust me when I say that even simple exchanges such as these required all my intuitive skills so that I could really assess Eliza's emotional state and respond with sensitivity. *Terrible* is a strong word to describe how you are doing. In the sometimes black-or-white emotional world of a teenager, we mothers need to respect the words that our daughters choose; however, we must not always take them literally. This simple mirroring, these initial mothering-as-martial-art moves of mine—in which I would keep my comments to a minimum, while also communicating my concern with a tender tone and not trying to fix her "terrible" right then and there—gave her the "space" to come back to me. My facial expressions, tone, and body language made as much of an impact as did my limited and carefully chosen words. And when I was in my martial-arts groove, my subtle moves almost always proved effective. Our first exchange of the afternoon, sensitively mirrored by me, made it easy for her to return later—sometimes just a few minutes later—to tell me why she was feeling or doing "terrible."

Mirroring your daughter need not be done perfectly (what a relief, since that's impossible). Not only is that an unattainable goal, but it would also be stifling for any human to be perfectly attuned to herself or to another. Our daughters actually need us to *not* be perfectly attuned; they need a degree of ineffectiveness from us so they can learn to deal with real-world frustration and to know where they start and you end. The conflicts and adjustments that you constantly have to make—think of Molly and Claire arguing over curfews—are actually useful grist for the mill; if your disagreements lead to clearer communication and better understanding, they can foster emotional growth, increase frustration tolerance, and help your daughter become an independent being. (I'm not joking here. I mean it.)

Winnicott offered the helpful notion that a mother only needs to be "good enough" in the first few years of a child's life. I suggest that we mothers cut ourselves some slack and apply that notion to mothering in adolescence, so that it might teach us the necessity of *not* being perfect. The messy reality of our imperfect life—and, yes, of our imperfect mothering—is actually necessary for our daughters' healthy growth. For example, admitting our mistakes to our daughter teaches her about the courage it takes to be vulnerable, how to live with integrity, and the idea that feeling humility is a mature accomplishment. In fact, if a mother does not admit her mistake and her daughter sees it (and what daughter does not see most of our mistakes), then that mother is not teaching her daughter to trust what she sees. "Fessing up" to our daughter is a form of mirroring her—and since she is likely to have seen our mistake anyway, we are giving her the gift of a reality check. Luckily, nobody's perfect. Or as my own teenage oracle once worked it out: we are all perfectly imperfect.

OUR CULTURE'S DISTORTED MIRROR

While we are with our daughters at home, we have quite a bit of influence over them. We can teach them to trust their intuition, we can encourage them to express their true feelings, and we can contain and mirror their emerging true selves. But how can we protect their individuality and encourage them to express it fully outside the home in a conformist, peer-oriented culture? How can we meet the challenges of raising a girl so that her life belongs to *her* and is not a performance for others? Our culture encourages our daughters to look externally, instead of internally, to find value and self-esteem, and to find identity and happiness from her body, her grades, and her material possessions. Thus, we often find ourselves swimming against the tide.

For nearly three decades, first as a nurse-practitioner and now as a therapist, I have been working with girls and women who struggle with body image, food, and eating disorders. I feel I have been taking the ever-strengthening pulse of an epidemic. As I seek to mirror one-on-one each girl and woman that I see, and to help her see her own soul underneath her pain and struggles, I also try to find a larger pattern to this harmful outbreak. What does it mean that so many millions of women and girls hate their bodies? As the young author Courtney E. Martin asks in her book *Perfect Girls, Starving Daughters* (written for and about Eliza's generation): Why is there such a frighteningly new normalcy in body hatred?

Some of this new normalcy must be a product of our broader worldview. We have learned to objectify (to view as a machine) the living, breathing miracle that is our body. In doing so, we lose the subjective experience of what it means to be a woman. True to our left hemisphere–dominated culture, we culturally sensitive women tend to miss the lovely forest of our whole beings, breaking our bodies into parts (trees) and evaluating them in isolation, as though our bodies were not integrated wholes. It is difficult to actually inhabit our bodies if we are trained to see our body parts separately and to view our bodies as objects—like pieces of sculpture that can be molded, manipulated, and "fixed" with diets, workouts, and cosmetic surgery. When their time comes, our young daughters may follow our culture's lead: "I hate my stomach," they may say. "My butt is too big, and it's not firm enough. I like my hands okay, but my hair is too thin, my hips are too wide, and my left breast is larger than my right breast." Believe it or not, our daughters are exposed to this kind of talk by the time they enter middle school (or before!), and all it takes is one girl's chatter for a brush fire to start in the classroom. Add to this the possibility that your daughter's teacher might be having a weight-loss contest with other teachers at her school, and you'll see how our daughters are surrounded by a culture of body obsession.

Martin describes one disturbing study in which a majority of teens and young women admitted that they would rather be hit by a truck than be fat![1] Knowing this, we ought to never, ever make another disparaging comment about our own thighs. Instead, we should consider another way to talk about our bodies and to be resolute in not contributing to this toxic environment.

This issue of body hatred, or even body dislike, may not be your issue or your daughter's issue. Congratulations and dance a jig! Seriously! But surely most of us can count on a single hand the number of women we know who actually *like* their bodies just as they are. And sadly, we might still have a finger or two left. Even if she doesn't have a problem with body image, what kind of influence is this mass hypnosis having on your daughter? Will we ever be able to mirror body acceptance for our daughters, let alone ourselves, among a female chorus of friends, family, and coworkers who "dis" their own bodies on a daily basis?

Despite all my training and experience as a therapist, all the healing I have done on my own body image over the years, and all the positive mirroring I did with Eliza as she grew into her womanly, curvaceous body, I still watched somewhat helplessly as she struggled with her own body image during middle school. She was never close to developing an eating disorder, but her meal-skipping behavior and her unhealthy attitudes were, in Courtney Martin's terms, frighteningly *normal.* Unless Eliza had been raised on a deserted island, I am not sure she could have avoided this painful rite of passage. What Eliza shares about body image and body trust with your girls (her chapter 4, pages 73–99) is essential reading for you as well.

So let's state the obvious once more: since your daughter is growing up female in this new kind of normal, it is likely that her self-esteem will depend to some degree on how she feels about her body. This is another reason that I believe you need to be at the center of your daughter's life: you need to mirror her soul with a love of your whole body and hers. If we leave it up to the culture at large, much less to her peer group, a distorted and immature mirror will reflect her. The mythically thin and unblemished perfect body image that your daughter finds in the cultural mirror is just one of the many unobtainable goals that Courtney Martin refers to in her book. She describes a kind of "de evolution" from mother to daughter as her Millennial peers aspire to ever-more unobtainable goals:

> Our mothers had the luxury of aspiring to be "good," but we have the ultimate goal of effortless perfection . . . We must not only be perfect—as in accomplished, brilliant, beautiful, witty— but also appear as if we achieve all this perfection through an easygoing, fun-loving approach . . . A starving daughter lies at the center of each perfect girl. The face we show to the world is one of beauty, maturity, determination, strength, willpower, and ultimately, accomplishment. But beneath the façade is a daughter—starving for attention and recognition, starving to justify her own existence.[2]

There is a deadly problem with *appearances* in the situation that Martin describes. The façade that Martin describes is what Winnicott named the False Self, an essential construct that he believed could either serve us or destroy us. According to Winnicott, in its healthy manifestation, the False Self is a necessary public mask that is polite and appropriate for many situations. In its pathological manifestation, however, the False Self complies with others' expectations to such a degree that it buries the True Self—the soul. You may have no agenda for your daughter other than that she become her truest self. Unfortunately, the culture at large is giving her a very different set of instructions, and we have the extremely difficult task of helping her discern what is her passion (her True Self) and what is her performance (her public mask). Adolescents are particularly prone to complying to cultural stereotypes and norms as they seek to build a mature identity. It will be tempting for your daughter to buy into the images of airbrushed perfection she sees everywhere—whether they be images of perfect bodies or perfect relationships or perfect accomplishments. Martin's call to action is that we be aware of this elusive and illusory goal of "effortless perfection" upon which our daughters might privately be setting their sights.

Even with a stronger sense of her False and True Selves, your daughter's task of standing strong among others her age is daunting. The magnitude of this task has led me to wonder how we can teach girls to be true to their individual souls and to value, express, and celebrate the uniqueness of their beings. I began asking what tools we could use to teach our daughters to love themselves from the inside, rather than accepting an external standard that does not take their deepest, most essential selves into consideration. And I wondered whether instead of being alone in this process, it would be possible for our girls to go through it together and with our guidance. Mirroring is definitely one step in teaching our girls to be true to themselves—to not betray themselves, their bodies, or each other.

RECOGNIZING RITES OF PASSAGE

Adolescence is a passage. If we remember that our daughters are making this passage from girls into women over the course of just a decade, then we might consider conscious ways to honor or mark (through celebration or ritual) the psychological, emotional, physiological, and spiritual growth they are achieving in this short kaleidoscopic span. What we commonly call a *rite of passage* is actually a ritual that honors the passage a person is making from one status in life to the next—in adolescence, or when they become a mother (baby showers), or in midlife (have you noticed that there are a lot of fortieth and fiftieth birthday celebrations happening these days?), or at life's end when we honor the passage of a soul "into the next world" with a memorial service or funeral.

A rite of passage can honor the death/rebirth cycle that is occurring in adolescence. Here is one way to consider what is happening with your adolescent daughter: As in the Vasilisa myth, her relationship with you, as you have known it, is "dying" or has "died." It is being "born" in a new form. In our workshops, I guide mothers in creating a simple rite (a ritual) that honors their daughter's imminent adolescent passage. It is a short and simple ritual, but it is very, very powerful. While the daughters are off with Eliza, I help the mothers make miniature girl-in-your-pocket dolls that they will give to their daughters. When the daughters return, many mothers are amazed by their daughter's absolute delight at receiving such a beautiful handmade gift that comes with their mother's loving words of reflection. And this ritual has lasting power: Eliza and I hear from daughters who tell us that they have kept and treasured this doll for many years and have proudly taken it "in their pocket" to college.

Many mothers I have worked with have created other ways to celebrate their daughter's passage into womanhood, because they see the value in this kind of initiation ritual, whether it is an afternoon tea with strawberry shortcake or a weekend away at a special place. Many have organized a gathering of the women who are most dear to their daughter—women who come with precious gifts of heirloom jewelry or inspiring books and, of course, hugs and words that bless the adolescent daughter's emerging self. And men can be there as well. Each family can and should find its own way of welcoming their daughters (and for that matter, their sons!) into adulthood.

Marion Woodman has said that without shared and recognized rites that have some useful form, members of a society are not sure who they are within the structure of that society. Many indigenous cultures had a clear set of instructions for adolescents, and puberty was acknowledged with a rite of passage shared among kin or entire communities. Unfortunately, we contemporary mothers are left to mirror our daughters at puberty with very limited resources. In our modern world, we need to somehow find creative alternatives to acknowledge our daughters' emerging womanhood so that they are not left, in Woodman's words, to "fumble their way through puberty."[3]

I am not saying that our daughters will fumble through puberty if we don't have an adolescent initiation ritual for them! But unfortunately, activities like clothes shopping and participation in Weight Watchers have become some of the more common modern rites of passage for our daughters. It is as if consumption and body-image conflicts have become some of the ways for adolescent girls to enter the women's club and share a modern woman's language. "Oh, no thank you, I'm on a diet," many teens learn to say. When women connect over the hatred of their bodies or their latest diet, or when millions of Americans are watching *The Biggest Loser* together, our girls may conclude that this is how women obtain a sense of belonging. Certainly there are better ways to give our daughters a sense of belonging, whether these ways are planned rituals or spontaneous encounters.

When my friend Caroline's daughter, Julia, was about twelve, she noticed that her belly was expanding. Julia said it looked as though a lifesaver was sitting on top of her hips, encircling her body. It was with some alarm that she said to her mother, "Look, Mom, I'm fat!" Julia knew she was already fairly unique among her friends: she was a creative introvert and a reader, and she loved nature. What she didn't know, until Caroline reassured her, was that her own nature was creating a lifesaver on her sweet belly, preparing a reserve for Julia's imminent growth spurt. Furthermore, the adipose tissue (um, that would be fat) on her belly was busy making estrogen so that she could become the beautiful twenty-three-year-old woman she is today.

But this story is really about how Caroline, who is an extrovert, a health coach, and an amazing mom, reassured Julia. To Julia's comment, "Look, Mom, I'm fat!" she responded, "Fat? Fantastic! Let me see your beautiful fat!" And she proceeded to explain to Julia what her beautiful and smart body was up to. In the same way that she would celebrate her daughter's first period a few months later, she celebrated the appearance of the lifesaver around her daughter's middle, and she made sure that Julia understood that the extra flesh was a portent of lovely female changes to come. Clearly, this "F" word was not a bad word in this family!

Although it might be hard for us to call fat *beautiful* given the prevalence of childhood obesity, consider the science: Our bodies have an innate wisdom. If they are fed healthy food in moderate amounts, they will naturally find their own genetic set-point, which includes a certain amount of fat on our hips. After all, fat on our body produces estrogen, which is the miracle hormone behind our strong bones and our fertility. The more we know about our remarkable feminine bodies, the more our daughters can be proud of theirs.

This everyday mirroring can start before puberty. I recently read a posting by a mother on Rachel's Blog (hosted by Rachel Simmons, author of *Odd Girl Out*) that illustrates another lovely spontaneous rite of passage. After unsuccessfully trying every rational "but you are beautiful" argument she could think of, this writer, the mother of a seven-year-old daughter grappling with her jiggly belly, tried something a little more radical:

> I stand her up on the step stool in front of the mirror. I strip off
> my yoga pants, my tee shirt, my bra and underwear. We are side
> by side, completely naked together. She laughs. I start singing a
> song that I'm making up as I go. It's rap meets Raffi, with lyrics like,
> "We are perfect, just the way we are." It's wild and silly, but I cannot
> be stopped. We're shaking everything, and she's belly laughing and
> totally thrilled. I pick her up. We are a ridiculous and magnificent
> pair . . . I carry her to the bedroom, raving about all the ways we
> are powerful and naked and women. We settle into comfy pajamas
> and read a story together. Fat is not mentioned again.
>
> On this night, I have no idea if I have succeeded. I'm not sure
> if what I said and did had an impact, if I fixed anything, or even if
> I changed her mind. But I do know that I must continue to infuse
> myself and my children with bold confidence. I must check in, ask
> questions, take the time. I must build and undo. I must be open
> and genuine. I must be willing to dance naked in the mirror . . .
> and stare straight into my reflection with love.[4]

It is a marvelous image, is it not? And though it may not be your way, I invite you to begin to imagine ways in which you might infuse bold confidence in your daughter. You can think of these ways as her rites of passage—whether they be teaching your daughter about the wisdom of her body storing a lifesaver on her midriff, or dancing naked with her in front of a mirror, or simply holding her close so she can *feel* your body's love for her perfectly imperfect body.

THE ARCHETYPAL MOTHER'S MIRRORING

At every workshop we lead, we pitch a lovely, lush red tent in a corner of our space as a place for moms and girls to go take breaks. We were inspired in part by Anita Diamant's novel *The Red Tent,* which tells the little-known biblical story of Dinah, daughter of the patriarch Jacob and his wife, Leah. In Genesis, Dinah does not say a single word, but Diamant imaginatively recasts the story and tells it from the fresh perspective of its women. The book's title refers to the tent in which women of Jacob's tribe must, according to ancient law, take refuge while menstruating or giving birth and in which they find mutual support and encouragement from their mothers, sisters, and aunts.

I confess that I've only recently let go of my cynicism about red tents and goddesses. The girls' delight in the red tent at our workshops has won me over. Our very simple, very feminine abode casts a spell of intimacy, pluckiness, and reverence that is hard to explain. The girls love the bright red and gold and pink brocade pillows made of luscious Indian fabrics, and the lanterns and the candles glowing at the table that holds a dozen images or so of goddesses from other cultures. Surrounded by our girls' artwork on the walls of the tent—images of their own newly anointed modern-day goddesses, such as the Goddess of Soup Kitchens and the Goddess of Bad Hair Days—all of us mothers are enchanted by the spell of the beautiful space our daughters have created. This experience is like a lovely rite reminiscent of those found in villages of old.

Inspired by the memory of their delight, I placed a beautiful miniature Green Tara, hand carved from wood, on my desk while I wrote this book. She is a Buddhist goddess who is considered a *bodhisattva* (an enlightened being, in the ancient Hindu language of Sanskrit) who was once a real person—just as the Buddha was once a real person named Prince Siddhartha and Jesus was a carpenter from Galilee. Among other gifts, she is the goddess of "enlightened action," and I imagined her helping me as I wrote. Occasionally I would look up to gaze at this colorful and curvaceous feminine figure, and she would fill me with a kind of purposeful delight.

Women and girls can gain great insight and sustenance by admiring an image of any kind in their female likeness, an image that is considered sacred. I have found that archetypal feminine images from different cultures and spiritual traditions have a way of seeping into our emerging feminine selves.

As a result, we might consider the holy matter that we live in—our own body—as our own private temple that holds our soul as we move through this life. In this temple—this funky little red tent of ourselves, all decorated and draped in our memories and images of our loved ones and ancestors and inspirations—we might find the strength to raise our daughters in a house where their feminine bodies are mirrored as the beautiful and sacred temples that they are.

"YOU ARE THE FAIREST OF THEM ALL!"

My definition of mothering—*raising your daughter to become herself*—has helped me remember to make mothering the daily practice of living my own life, so that Eliza is free to live hers. Jung once said, "The greatest burden a child must bear is the unlived life of the parent,"[5] and I have worked at separating out my version of who I think Eliza *should* be from who she is and who she is becoming. In the fairy tale *Snow White*, it is a positive "mothering" mirror that finally tells Snow White the truth—that she is the fairest of them all. A mother who is living her own life is not threatened by her daughter's inner or outer beauty; to this kind of mother, while her daughter's beauty is not an extension of her, it is her delight!

As Marion Woodman puts it:

> A mother who honors her own body and her own soul can create
> a clear mirror for her child. Through her, the child learns that *her*
> own body is her soul's home on this earth, that it has respected
> boundaries, and that its feelings and needs are recognized.
> Instead of using the child to mirror her, as some mothers do with
> disastrous results, the conscious mother mirrors the essence of her
> child—its delight, its anger, its imagination.[6]

I would add to this list "its beauty." And with this priceless gift of clear mirroring from her mother, a daughter, steadily over time, learns that it is safe to become her *self.*

5

Inside Every Mother
Is a Daughter

Every mother contains her daughter in herself and every daughter her mother, and
every mother extends backwards into her mother and forwards into her daughter.
—C. G. JUNG

LONG AGO, A RUSSIAN FRIEND of mine gave me a set of twelve
Russian nesting dolls   twelve of them! These brightly colored and so-very-
female *matryoshka* dolls are still among my favorite possessions. The first
doll is quite large, perhaps ten inches tall, and the last one is so small it is
like a little embryo, miraculously dressed in the same beautiful clothes as all
the "women" who have come before her. Even if you've never seen a young
girl play with a set of matryoshkas, it's not hard to imagine her delight as
she puts together and takes apart the "generations" of wooden dolls.

I love my nesting dolls, because they are beautiful, because they remind
me of my friend, and because they are a concrete representation of the
observation of Jung's that opens this chapter—an image of safe containment and holding. They embody the idea that generations from the past
can *contain* us by giving us a feeling of security, a feeling of knowing who
we are by knowing where we have come from. For me, they also represent
the kind of healthy psychological containment that we mothers can carry
within our own psyches and therefore pass on to our daughters.

Some mothers come from a long line of pain and disconnection, where
the nesting dolls are fractured or don't fit so neatly or so safely inside of

each other. Even if you have a painful or unworkable relationship with your mother, or if your matriline is marred by trauma of any kind, I believe you can connect to this idea of finding and creating a safe and healthy containment for you and your daughter. Perhaps you have already been making this idea a reality in your life.

Containing, like mirroring, is a concept that has been essential to me over the two decades that I have been a mother. The concept is one that can be difficult to grasp at first, as it may seem a little too theoretical for some. But once understood, it is consummately useful. Essentially, containing means creating a safe environment, complete with both emptiness and boundaries, in which a person can *be*. The emptiness allows space for people to experience themselves in all of their different moods and emotional states, while the boundaries create security. As parents, containing is exactly what we want to do: allow our children the space to be and become who they are, while also providing the boundaries that will keep them safe, both physically and psychologically, as they do so.

CONTAINING BASICS

Conscious mothering is about mothering our daughters so that they may take root in the open field of the world in their own way, all the while recognizing that there are many ways for them to be rooted, grounded, and contained. In fact, from the very beginning of our relationship with them, when they were literally rooted inside of us with umbilical cords (or if you adopted your daughter, when you first "conceived" of her), we have been containing our precious girls. The uterus is the original feminine container, the first place in which a life is protected so that it might safely grow. It is a soft and nourishing vessel.

Imagine that in an ideal world, you go from one safe vessel to the next. What is the next safe vessel available to your baby daughter after she emerges from the womb? She lies naturally in your loving arms, of course. At some point thereafter, you recognize that she also needs to be psychologically contained, a process that is built upon the symbiotic relationship that occurs between mother and child at birth. *Symbiosis,* defined psychologically, can include the natural, beneficial merging of a mother's and infant's psyches following birth. This period of closeness is necessary so that the mother can optimally respond to the needs of a being unable to care for itself in any way. We can look at symbiosis as the first out-of-the-womb containing that we do as mothers. And just as our precious infant is dependent on us for food and shelter, she is also dependent on us for containing our frustration and fatigue if she is a "fussy" or even colicky baby. Our patience becomes a container for her. Our patience holds her as surely as our arms do. And our patience will be tested when she becomes a toddler.

Our toddler has a psychological birth full of the "contractions" of stranger anxiety and tantrums, as well as the thrill of pushing the limits of one's comfortable confines and toddling off into the bigger world. Pushing the limits at this age is not defiance—it is the normal and natural behavior that is *required* in order for each child to begin the journey of becoming an autonomous human being. Understanding what is going on developmentally with our toddler is another form of containment. Assuming that we aren't narcissistic, we don't become dependent on our child's dependence. In other words, we are not overly identified with our role as a mother, because we ourselves have psychologically individuated. We do not need to keep our children reliant on us longer than is necessary, because we have a healthy sense of who *we* are. When our daughters know that we are not threatened by their moving out into the world, they feel psychologically safe to do so. As our child's world gets larger and larger, our love and encouragement can hold her as she starts to sense the fragile beginnings of her own identity, her own ego, her own thoughts and feelings—her own *self.*

I find it useful to think of parenting as the practice of holding a safe psychological and emotional container for our children to grow in. The parent's job is to continue to adjust and readjust and enlarge and strengthen this container as the child matures developmentally. Conscious mothering is having the awareness that we are "holding" and monitoring (at gradually more and more of a distance) our child's progress. When your daughter has a tantrum as a toddler, your job as a mother is to contain that tantrum, both literally and psychologically. Our children look to us to learn emotional regulation. If we can't handle and allow for our emotions, how will our children ever learn to feel comfortable in their own emotional states? You must make sure, as your child is flailing around, that she does not hit her head on the corner of a table or trip on a hurled toy. Just as important, you must hold the understanding that tantrums are a normal part of development, and like storms, they will pass. Your patient presence demonstrates to your toddler that you can be depended on to not be drawn into the tantrum or to take it personally. That way, when your toddler comes out of the tantrum, she can experience your steadiness and incorporate it into her growing sense of self. She may have fallen apart, but her world has not. Mother is still standing and ready to contain her exhausted little girl in her arms to reassure her that all is well again with the world.

When your adolescent daughter is "falling apart," it is a whole other kind of storm. But even though the weather system of a teenage girl—because of her sheer size and vocabulary—may be overwhelming, if we understand her growth process, we can find the patience necessary to keep standing and to still be standing as she makes her way to the other side of her storm system. Many developmental psychologists compare the "second birth" of toddlers to a "third birth" in adolescence. Like toddlers, adolescents must explore, test limits, and become autonomous—and they have tantrums! Adolescents, unlike toddlers, must commit to an identity or sense of self if their psychological birth is to be successful. This means that different roles, behaviors, and ideologies must be tried out in order to select an identity. Your adolescent daughter, in essence, is trying to figure out *who she is,* and sometimes it can feel to her as if she is "falling apart."

If you fundamentally know who *you* are, your daughter will have a strong container in which to land during adolescence. Your healthy psyche becomes her next safe vessel as she begins to explore her own independent identity. Conscious mothering means that you are paving the way, so to speak, for your daughter. As Dr. Christiane Northrup writes in her book *Mother-Daughter Wisdom:*

> Books such as *Reviving Ophelia, Saving Beauty from the Beast, Queen Bees & Wannabes, Odd Girl Out,* and *Girlfighting* have elucidated the cultural context that puts so many adolescent girls at risk. But that's only one part of the story. Daughters don't become "unconscious" in the areas in which their mothers are fully conscious. Ophelia won't need reviving if her mother has already been resuscitated—or never needed resuscitation in the first place. Beauty is less likely to fall for the Beast if her self-esteem is high and if her mother has taught her how to be in touch with her instincts.[1]

A mother's awareness of her own instincts—an awareness that is born out of her experience—is a psychological container for her daughter. And if you are beginning to feel anxious because you are not a wise, patient, steady, and conscious container for your daughter 100 percent of the time—in other words, you are not perfect—please take a breath and cut yourself some slack. As I stated in chapter 4, perfection is not a desirable goal for a mother or for anyone else. Part of being an adult is making mistakes and having the maturity to repair those mistakes. This means that we apologize when it is appropriate and that we teach our daughters what psychologists call the "rupture and repair" cycle, which is essential in healthy and strong relationships.

Not only do you not have to make the "right" or "best" choice every time you face a parenting decision (though making good choices much of the time is what we strive for), you also don't have to give your children your hyperfocused attention all the time. Studies have shown that children actually thrive when we are not "perfectly" present. Yes, they thrive when we are available, but we don't have to be "on" all the time, and we don't have to keep them constantly busy with purposeful, creative projects. To be off to the side, humming away in another room, or perhaps working on our own projects—to be living a life *we* love—is what our daughters need from us to hold them as they grow.

The essence of what I am saying is this: You need to be the adult in your relationship with your daughter. Your emotional maturity is a container for your daughter as she learns how to navigate the new and intense feelings that come with adolescence. Without this maturity, you will be the blind grown-up leading the blind child.

HOLDING THE LINE

One of the ways that the container of my emotional maturity could lose some of its holding power was when my teenage girl challenged the limits her dad and I had established regarding her social life and safety. It was hard for me to stay firm and consistent. I'm guessing you can relate. Once a curfew was set or a cell-phone time limit was determined, Eliza would invariably push for more social freedom. It took lots of discipline and resolve on my part to trust our decisions about the limits we had set and to not give in to my charming and clever daughter's multiple strategies:

"Please, Mom, just this one time?" she would ask. First there would be a smile or a hug, and then promises, and then finally, her pleas. It was hard for me to hold firm against her sometimes amusing—and, yes, always pretty annoying—onslaughts. I can't tell you how tempting it was, in the moment, to give in. I admit that an immature (and irrational) part of me worried that she wouldn't love me anymore if I didn't say yes. And many times her arguments actually made rational sense. "Well, yes, I see her point," I might think in the middle of one of her onslaughts. "I can't really disagree with that." How she worked away at me, and at the same time, how I worked at keeping my inner resolve! I was successful at not using the parenting refrain from my parents' generation: "Because I said so!" Eventually, after explaining my reasoning for the second or third time, I would come to the end of my rope and my refrain became: "Enough, Eliza; ENOUGH!"

Sometimes I had to actually step away from the situation in order to bolster my resolve and contain *myself*. I would say something like, "Eliza, hammering at me like this is not going to help your cause. I have an errand to run [or a phone appointment, or a meeting to go to, or another child to pick up], and I'll be back in twenty minutes. When I get back, no more discussion about this." My twenty-minute break from her badgering allowed me to take a few deep breaths and get some perspective. If I felt I was beginning to change my mind about a limit that I knew we needed to keep, I'd call my husband or a friend for support in staying the course, and have them contain and mirror me. Little by little, it became easier for me to hold my own—it was another mothering-as-a-martial-arts dance step I learned along the way.

If removing yourself from the situation isn't viable or doesn't appeal to you, find a different strategy, one that works for you. And a postscript: there were quite a few times that Eliza even ended up thanking me—not immediately, but later—for standing firm. And even if your daughter does not admit it or is unaware of it, I guarantee you that she craves your limit setting, as well as your consistency with adhering to those limits.

WHAT ARE YOUR CONTAINERS?

If you're beginning to get a sense that your daughter needs safe containment, that's good. But that's only half of it. You need safe containment, too. When we mothers are contained, we can more readily carry our daughters through the ups and downs of adolescence. In addition to the important relationships in your life, what other containers—literal, psychological, emotional, and spiritual—rejuvenate you and keep you steady and centered? How do they help you be the adult in the relationship, the emotionally mature mother upon whom your teenage daughter can rely?

If you have a close relationship with your mother, then she is a container that "holds" you, just as you "hold" your daughter—quite like the Russian dolls I described. Grandmothers, aunts, and godmothers can be the essential arms that hold us—both literally and figuratively—and sometimes sustain us as we mother our adolescent daughters. Many of these women have "been there," and their love and advice are crucial. Who are the wise women in your life—the mentors—whom you can depend on? Marion Woodman mentored me and many other women, and we all feel as if we are her daughters. She never had any biological children, but every year on Mother's Day, her home is filled with flowers that are sent to her from far and wide. We, her students, have felt "held" by her, contained by her, even at a distance.

I have already talked about knowledge of and pride in our female ancestry as a container. A religious or spiritual path can hold us as well—our god (or goddess), a 12-step program, yoga, prayer, or meditation. Nature in all its beauty can restore us, inspire us, and hold us. Our values are an essential and strong parenting container. Values that are rooted and easily articulated strengthen us and give us the certainty we need when we are setting limits for our teenage daughters. Our instincts, as Dr. Northrup says, are where we need to be rooted so that our daughter can find her way to *her* instincts, which are another sure container. If we can't trust our own values and instincts, how will she trust hers? Our body is literally our container, and if we can't love and trust and take care of our own body, how will she do the same for hers?

Recently I received a letter from a mother named Jennifer who had been at a Mothering & Daughtering weekend six months before. While at our workshop at the Omega Institute, she had taken a couple of yoga classes for the first time. She continued this practice once she returned home, and she couldn't believe the difference it was making in her life. Her stress had been greatly reduced, and she was sleeping better. The consistency of her yoga practice was helping her to be more consistent in her care of her twelve-year-old daughter, Chloe. Consistency is a container. She was actively taking care of herself—"mothering" herself—which helped provide her with the inner resources she needed to mother her daughter.

Does this sound too simple? I'm *not* suggesting that practicing yoga a couple times a week will miraculously transform your relationship with your daughter. Jennifer was also doing plenty of self-reflection and some important internal healing work. I *am* saying that if you know you can count on yourself to take care of yourself, it is much easier to count on yourself to take care of your daughter, too. And when you take care of yourself, you are more resilient.

Your adolescent daughter is watching how you carry yourself through life. In fact, more than just watching, she is scrutinizing—as you may have already discovered, much to your chagrin. You are her mother and her mentor, and she is imprinting your behavior. It is crucial that you find sources of replenishment so that you can return to the task of mothering her in a renewed and refreshed way. A relationship with a partner, husband, friend, therapist, sibling, or parent can be an essential source of replenishment, a container to "hold" you, both literally and figuratively. Wisdom and courage are other containers. Joy is a container. Being financially secure is a container—something that I will discuss in more depth in the next chapter. Whatever strengthens your sense of self, your confidence, and your capacity to consciously mother can be a container to hold and support you, so that you can hold and carry her with strength and self-assurance. These containers become what carry you, so that you can carry her.

Honoring the Matriline as a Container

"Welcome everyone, I am Priscilla. I'm Eliza's mother. I am also the daughter of Alden, who is the daughter of Priscilla, who was the daughter of Anabel, who was the daughter of Anna." This is how I introduce myself in the opening circle of our workshops. I could recite the names of many generations of my motherline, a rarity in our country of immigrants, but I stop where it feels natural, with my great-great-grandmother, Anna, the lovely and feisty pioneer who settled with her husband in upstate New York. I stop with her because I can remember my mother talking about Anna, and the stories I heard about her made her very real for me. When I am done with my introduction, it is Eliza who goes next, repeating our lineage from her standpoint.

Most of the women in the workshop know the names of two or three generations of mothers who have come before them, and each mother introduces herself as I have done, and then her daughter follows. From mother to daughter, to the next mother and then her daughter, we meet each other in a symphony of female names. At first, most of the girls are reluctant to jump in. Likely they haven't thought about their granny out in Seattle in a while, let alone *her* mother—known only, perhaps, as a stoic, gray-haired lady looking up from the pages of a photo album. But by the time we get rolling on these royal-sounding introductions, the girls are very focused and inquisitive, even reverential. It doesn't take much to awaken their interest—clearly there is some form of magic in this invocation. For myself, I imagine we've built an invisible and collective spiritual container as we each honor the women who have given us life, even if there is pain in our matriline. We've created our own set of living, breathing matryoshka dolls.

In our modern world, we may know the names of some of our female ancestors, but we are lucky if we know their stories beyond "she had six children" or "her husband died in the war, and she was left to raise her family on her own" (defining them in terms of others and not themselves). Indeed, we are fortunate in this country if we have a few faded photographs that give us a hint of our female ancestors' hopes and fears. Eliza's knowledge of many generations of women (and men) in our family is the result of my father's interest in genealogy. In the beginning of a book that he lovingly put together and dedicated to his grandchildren, he placed the following Chinese proverb: "To forget one's ancestors is to be a brook without a source, a tree without roots." I am grateful to him for doing the work that allows me to feel my roots and connect to my source. The luxury of time and literacy has allowed for this ancestral memory, something not possible for many of us until this past century. For others, it's still not possible.

If you or your daughter is adopted, you have two matrilines that you can honor—both the biological one (often represented by the biological culture) and the adoptive mother's. Kelsey was a single mother at one of our workshops who made a practice of grounding herself and her adopted daughter, Alice, with visits to Alice's first "mother" country, China. Even though Alice did not know the female names of her ancestors there, she came to know the rich Chinese culture and celebrated one of her lineages by being in the country of her birth. Kelsey had decided to take Alice to China every five years, and so they had gone when she was five and then ten. Now, at fourteen, Alice was looking forward to celebrating this part of her heritage once again the following year. Kelsey wanted to help root Alice in a meaningful past that included returning to and being surrounded by the faces, the language, the countryside, and even the food of her ancestors. And clearly, the ritual trip held deep meaning for Alice.

There are others, as well, who may want to celebrate two matrilines—daughters with two lesbian mothers, for example, and daughters with both a mother and a particularly close stepmother. Daughters without a mother who are being raised by a father, grandmother, aunt, or godmother will also have both biological and emotional-psychological matrilines to explore. We can all find ways to honor different motherlines. We are fortunate to live in an age in which family and ancestry are beginning to be defined and celebrated in new and diverse ways.

In Western cultures, most families are not rooted in the memory of their ancestors' names and stories. Elsewhere in the world, however, the collective memory is extensive. In West African traditions, for example, a local *griot* (pronounced GREE-oh), or the village's storyteller, musician, and oral historian, records in memory and song the births, deaths, marriages, and cultural traditions of generations of village families. Names and stories are kept alive in the ritual retelling through song of the tribe's or community's history. What does it do for a culture to have a consciousness of its roots that extends back so many hundreds of years? What does it do for a young person to have his or her village's memory in music and song expressed with beauty and celebration?

In older European cultures, meticulous written records and a strong sense of the past give people a rootedness that is unfamiliar to us Americans. Many of our ancestors arrived here essentially penniless but full of the hope of creating a new life and new traditions. Later, immigrants often assimilated into the American culture quickly, which frequently meant Anglicizing or shortening the family name. Many stopped speaking in their mother tongue in order to help their children assimilate as easily as possible. Others deliberately chose to "forget" their ancestral relatives. Although America has offered us the opportunity to reinvent ourselves and create a new culture, we Americans have also endured a great uprooting. Many of us are not grounded or contained by a meaningful past. This is true particularly among women and girls, as our history has left out so many of the stories of women. I am convinced that the omission of tales of the unsung heroines among women in history—the challenges they faced and the hardships they endured—is one source of the difficulty that girls now have in honoring and respecting the lineage of their motherline. In addition, a lack of grounding in our own personal female ancestors' stories renders it more challenging for us to find compassion for the limitations of the women who have come before us.

When Eliza and I come together with groups of mothers and daughters, we suggest that we are taking root together as we look at our matrilines and weave a tapestry of our ancestors' names. Each mother takes the griot's role, and she passes on her "song" of female names to her daughter, who in turn learns that song. We become rooted in our weekend community, as we speak these names of mothers and grandmothers and great-grandmothers. We invite everyone to place photographs of their ancestors and any women who are important to them—teachers, mentors, aunts, and sisters—on a table. The mothers and daughters write notes; they leave a locket or a flower. In the encouragement of these acts, we are gently teaching our daughters to honor their ancestors and the important women in their lives. We do this as a way for them to symbolically carve one precious container for themselves—an enduring container, one they can pass on to their daughters someday. On page 147 of our shared chapter 7, you and your daughter will have the opportunity to do an exercise for connecting to your matriline right at home.

Community as a Container

Where is Marika? Her mother, Cynthia, really needs to know. Had something recently eaten her brain? What used to be giggly get-togethers and sleepovers for Marika and her friends has overnight become a preference for friendship at a distance. Hundreds of friends on Facebook are literally not enough for Marika. Texting is the new connecting, and her chatter has sped up. Cynthia is concerned that the quantity of virtual "friends" has suddenly replaced the quality of real friendship.

Of equal concern to Cynthia is that Marika's once good grades have plummeted, and she no longer wants to play the clarinet—something Marika had felt passionate about just a year earlier. "She has no passion except to stay connected on the Internet every waking hour!" Cynthia feels so desperate about Marika's situation that she is considering sending her away to boarding school—something she would have never imagined only a few months earlier.

Cynthia's feeling of helplessness is further compounded by the fact that most of the parents in her community don't share her values and set far fewer limits with their children than she does with Marika. Cynthia also bemoans the fact that she does not know most of Marika's friends' parents. Unlike Cynthia, the other parents work nine to five or later, and have little time or opportunity to become the "village" to help raise one another's children. Cynthia laments, "After a while, Marika wears me down. She pleads with me and tells me that I am the only mother who sets limits. At least at boarding school, there would be a contained environment and agreed-upon rules that everyone has to follow."

In the five years that I have been teaching Mothering & Daughtering workshops, I have watched mothers move from concern to alarm as social media and technology develop ever-more seductive and effective ways for our teenagers to stay in touch without actually being together in community. Recent research warns us that too much time on the Internet can effect our adolescent children's brain development, and texting is addictive and can affect attention span and social skills. And although these technologies can help us to stay in touch with our daughters—which is a wonderful thing—they can also prevent us from having real, in-person contact and connections with our family and community. Who would have thought we might be longing for the days when we watched television together as families! But now that we are in separate rooms, glued to our computers, communal viewing of "the idiot box," as my parents used to call it, seems more and more appealing. We have lost touch with each other in the most fundamental and relational sense. Our "hearth" is no longer a fireplace or even a TV—we are isolated in front of these strange portals to elsewhere. As I look backward on my matriline, I wonder what my many grandmothers, particularly those who lived before the Industrial Revolution, would make of our very peculiar and unnatural behavior.

But how quickly we can have each other back. Twenty-four hours into a recent workshop, it was hard to believe that most of us had felt so removed from the experience of a close-knit community just days before. It was a crisp, clear Saturday night in October. Most of the mothers and daughters had come to our optional pajama party, and we mothers, sitting in a circle, watched in disbelief as our daughters braided each others' hair, made friendship bracelets, played card games, drew glorious goddesses for our red tent—all with mellow folk music playing in the background. We were in awe of our daughters' capacity to unhook from their cyberworld so quickly and completely, to connect with each other, and to have some good old-fashioned fun. Many of the mothers became instant converts to this way of being and were committed to returning to our imperfect communities with new energy and ideas for staying connected.

Hillary is a mother who tells us that she and her husband have had enough. They have searched for and found a town in Pennsylvania where a close-knit community still exists. Their uprooting was tough, but they have landed well, and their daughter and son now attend a Quaker school where they are thriving. Susanna has remained where she is with her fourteen-year-old daughter, Melanie, and has organized a group of mothers who meet regularly. They have created a community center for their teenagers as an alternative to their only other "town center"—the mall. Similarly, Katya tells us that a summer camp has "saved" her daughter Emily from "social death by alienation," and she wishes there were a way to re-create locally what Emily experiences only two months of the year.

Being surrounded by a community of friends or family, a "village" that raises your daughter and also holds *you,* is an essential container, but one that remains ever-more difficult to find in our mobile culture. It is staggering to recall how recently most of us lost the safe vessel of a familiar village or neighborhood life. This is a dramatic break from our own lengthy, pre-industrial past, as well as from mothers and daughters in "underdeveloped" countries, where familiarity and belonging are a reliable backdrop for one's personal narrative and growth. Until recently, the container for most mothers and daughters tended to be family life and the communal productivity of family farms or small family shops. Laborers and distant relatives were often parts of our households, and the elderly did not become segregated in retirement communities or nursing homes. Instead, they lived out their days within the family they'd been a part of all their lives.

It is foolish to romanticize these earlier times. Personal freedom, both for non-Caucasians and for women, was severely limited in ways that we would not find tolerable today. I would certainly not trade my life for any of the lives of my many generations of grandmothers—I love my freedoms and the fact that I have so many choices available to me. But therein lies the challenge of our age: to have infinite choices and yet so few worthy containers to put them in. We mothers, therefore, need to be selective. Our task, or one of our tasks, is to create environments in which our daughters can experience the security of familiarity and belonging without sacrificing our freedoms.

On that Saturday night, we mothers agreed that we could never give up the rights and freedoms that our female ancestors had not been privileged to enjoy. But we also agreed that something essential has been lost and therefore the quality of our daughters' lives is at risk, as is the quality of our relationship with them. Many of us are no longer contained by unchanging, familiar connections, by homey surroundings, and by the known rhythms of nature. There is no time for nonproductive pleasures; naps, daydreaming, and other idle pastimes no longer fit into the fast pace of our lives. The opportunity for a daughter to visit her grandmother next door, chatting the afternoon away as they bake a pie together, is less and less likely. More likely, Grandmother lives in another state and works for a living, and the pie recipe is put away or lost forever.

Modern life puts a pressure on us mothers to build the container of safety, support, and love that extended family and community formerly helped provide. There is no going back to the old order of things. We must find ways to build new communities based on old principles. We must use our creative minds and our caring hearts to feel our way through the dark and to bring our daughters along with us.

In the end, the greatest container of all is a loving heart. The experience of being loved—and in turn of loving ourselves for who we are—allows us to strengthen our psychic containers and return to the task of mothering our teenage daughters from our best selves. Surely this is what our female ancestors must have wanted for us, above all else.

6

Demeter's Determination

Unwilling to accept this state of affairs, Demeter rages and withholds
fertility from the earth until her daughter is returned to her. What
is important for women in this story is that the mother fights for
her daughter and for her relationship with her daughter.
—CAROL CHRIST

THERE ARE MANY DIFFERENT VERSIONS of the ancient Greek myth dedicated to Demeter and her daughter, Persephone, but few differ when it comes to the role of Hades, the possessive and forceful god of the underworld. Most ancient people seem to have agreed that Hades abducted and raped the maiden Kore, and thus the "initiated" Kore became "his" Queen Persephone.

Eliza has a very different tale to tell in her adaptation of the Demeter and Persephone myth (see page 129 of the Daughtering side). If you haven't read her version yet, it's time to read it now. For one thing, to this modern daughter of mine, Hades is not a rapist—he's more like a "hot" teenage boy. (Yikes!) Her maiden Kore goes willingly into the underworld, because she thinks Hades is "cute." To Eliza, liking boys was just one of the attractions of the underworld—which, in her version of the myth, she calls the "otherworld." From my perspective as a mother, this "otherworld" is just the new and exciting life beyond Eliza's "motherworld." It's a world where we mothers do not live or hold sway, and it is full of adventure, new experiences, and things that will make some of us mothers (myself included) feel uncomfortable—even alarmed—from time to time. No doubt, our daughters will venture into this

89

new realm, where they are in search of a new identity, just as the young maiden Kore ventured into a new realm and became Queen Persephone. The question for mothers is this: From whom will our daughter take her cues as she attempts to find a mature identity—from her peers or from us?

I maintain that it needs to be from us. But with the peer-oriented teen culture we all now live in, most mothers will need Demeter's determination in order to create and maintain a connected and steady—albeit shifting—relationship with their daughters. I've come to believe that if our girls have a strong bond with us, they will have the wisdom to navigate their social lives in the underworld and to not lose themselves to the conformist culture they will find there. In other words, if we protect our relationship bond with our daughter and give her plenty of ongoing assistance, she will stand a very good chance of being true to her emerging self, despite the temptations in the underworld to be anything but.

Eliza's version of the myth does not include what, for me, is one of the most important parts of the story—the mother's experience! After Persephone is abducted, Demeter searches day and night for her. And because Demeter is the goddess of the harvest, the seasons are halted, and all living things cease to grow as she wanders the earth in search of her beloved girl. Faced with the extinction of all life on earth, Zeus, the supreme god and ruler of Olympus, has no choice but to return Persephone to her mother. Without a doubt, it is Demeter's unwavering dedication to her daughter that forces this conclusion.

Reading from a modern-day mother's perspective, I see Demeter going to the ends of the earth to maintain her bond with her daughter. She fights for her daughter and doesn't stop fighting until she knows her girl is safe. Demeter is the original Mama Bear—her love is vast, and her commitment is fierce. I think you can probably relate, yes? I am encouraging you to trust your intuition and to do whatever it takes to make sure your bond with your daughter—and *her bond with you*—remains strong.

Note that it is Persephone, and not Kore, who is returned to Demeter. Demeter's daughter has changed; she has been in the business of finding her own life. But finding her own life does not mean that she leaves her mother behind. Eliza has left out this portion of the story, because from her perspective, well, sure, Persephone misses her mom, but she is busy finding her own way in the otherworld. The whole "mom thing" is just not as important as the whole adventure thing is. Know that this is very likely your daughter's perspective, too.

And then there are the pomegranate seeds. Many versions of the myth tell us that the new Queen Persephone *chooses* to eat the six pomegranate seeds that Hades offers her, which ensures that she can stay in the otherworld with her king for half the year. Others tell us that Hades tricks her into eating them. In any case, every year, with the advent of spring, Persephone returns to her mother with the mark of the otherworld on her lips. Our daughters, like Persephone, will leave us, but they will return. We must adjust to their comings and goings. Demeter, like us, maintains a steady home base, both literally and figuratively. She can do so because a mother's love—let's admit it—is enduring.

If you haven't read all of Eliza's Daughtering side of our book, go ahead and do so. In addition to defining *daughtering* and urging your daughter to remain intimate with you, Eliza mentors your daughter about the value of trusting her intuition, living authentically, and having trustworthy friends, to name just a few topics. One could say that she is meeting your daughter in the otherworld, where they have a shared teenage language, so that the two of them can bond. And their bonding will help your daughter trust Eliza when she tells your daughter how essential it is that she maintain a close relationship with you. Let's look at Eliza's *daughtering* definition once again. It speaks to the importance of this relationship most clearly:

> *Daughtering:* Being active in your relationship with your mom
> so that she knows the real you; balancing your independence with
> a dependable bond as you grow into your true self

Even with Eliza's mentoring, however, your daughter will be inclined to forget how essential her relationship is with you. Because she is being actively wooed by the attachment competition of her peers and she is getting a pretty direct message from our culture that she doesn't need you much, you must stay ever-more determined.

Staying determined will help you remember that the relationship between mother and daughter is not equal, nor should it be—at least not during adolescence. It is not your daughter's "job" to contain and mirror you, or to keep the attachment competition at bay, or to be the adult in your relationship. Even if you and your daughter are extremely close, it is natural for her to be thinking less about you than you are thinking about her. That is the nature of the mother–adolescent daughter relationship. Take it from Demeter—our daughters are always on our minds and in our hearts, and they will often take this (and us) for granted. That's okay. As they mature, they will come to appreciate us more and more. For now, it will be up to you to remain fiercely determined to keep the bond mutually strong.

RETRIEVING PERSEPHONE

Mothers who are able to stay near the center of their teen daughters' lives often need a little inspiration (or a lot of it) to help them keep their commitment strong. When you need to be reminded that all of your effort is worth it, think back on these words of Natalie, the mother of fourteen-year-old Lorna:

> I just wanted you to know that Lorna and I rediscovered each
> other at the workshop, and we have been closer these past few
> weeks than we have been in years. It is amazing to watch her open
> up with me about so many of her inner struggles. She has a new
> skip in her step! Yesterday, she asked me, "Mom, why did you
> let me go?" I was about to tell her that she had let me go, and I
> stopped myself. I realized that it was my responsibility to keep her
> close. I will not let this happen again!

All mothers and their daughters need more than an occasional weekend away to get or stay bonded through this period of life. Whether or not our daughters need retrieval from the underworld, preventive action for keeping our kids close has become necessary in our culture. Whether it is camping, periodic weekend trips, unintended breaks, or planned shared experiences that draw us into direct relationship, this bonding time is necessary. Most mothers will say that they cannot find a week or even a weekend in their own or their daughter's schedules, and many are reluctant to use precious resources to pay for a vacation. But depending on your own assessment of the state of your bond, you may not be able to afford *not* to take some time away together. And where *retrieval* is the word that fits your vision of what is needed, we must be fierce (like Demeter) and think radically and outside the box about solutions. For some mothers, this retrieval may require that they take their daughter out of school (with homework assignments in hand), usually with their daughter resisting every step of the way. For others, it might mean finding a whole day or a weekend with few social distractions and an agreement to have little or no access to phones, the Internet, or TV. Where there's a will, there's a way, and this investment in time (and money, perhaps) will pay off! Eliza and I both recommend that you ask your daughter to be involved in planning your time together—maybe even let your daughter come up with the plan for a weekend away or a shared activity.

In our case, I believe that our family's annual vacation to a cabin in the woods on an island in Maine, with no electricity or Internet access, was a mysterious key to our success in staying close. As much of a stretch financially as it was for us to maintain our access to the cabin every year, it somehow seemed essential to keeping us in balance together. A remote vacation like this surely sounds too challenging for some parents to imagine. Faced with such a desert of stimulation for modern teenagers, most parents wonder how their kids would spend their time away from video games, the Internet, phones, and friends—and how they would get enough of a break from their bored kids.

I do understand this conundrum. During a quiet vacation like this, it's likely that the whole family will face their addiction to the plugged-in-to-the Internet world we are all part of. My husband and I had to unplug in this desert of stimulation as well. I also wanted time away from mothering on our vacations, especially when Eliza was little. Sometimes all I wanted was to go on a vacation by myself. But I learned that my feelings of being overwhelmed while I was on vacation were a sign that I was not giving myself enough free time the other fifty weeks of the year, so I began to change that. I also came to realize that it was worth the investment of immersing myself in quality time with Eliza on our vacations—not only was it wonderful when I relaxed and let go, but it also paid off over the *entire year* after we returned home.

Without an investment of quality time with our adolescent daughters, we can't expect to automatically have a strong bond with them. Just as a relationship with a partner or a spouse or a close friend requires regular upkeep to maintain a strong bond and to keep communication open, so it is with our relationships with each of our children.

Being unplugged from the world once a year also gave Eliza a portal into her own creative inner life. She came to value her time with our family of three as *her* time. She anticipated and then savored the quiet, slowed-down pace of being with just herself and us, away from the world and its pressures. Once back home, it was our family dinners that seemed to be where we took our daily vacation from our overscheduled lives. We could talk and laugh about our day and enjoy our meal together. So dinner preparation and eating and talking about delicious food together became a reliable bonding ritual for our family. Somewhere along the way, being a "foodie" became a part of Eliza's teen identity. However, there is no way to separate these habits from our quiet times together in the cabin, away from it all—where, during one lovely afternoon of doing nothing, Eliza and I got the mad idea of writing a book together about mothering and daughtering.

Every family can find its own way of coming together. Since we all need to eat dinner, that's often the easiest logistically, even if dining together every night isn't possible. Attending religious services together offers another opportunity to spend regular, unplugged time together. We know one mother-daughter pair who knit together, another pair who go to yoga classes together, and still another pair who love going to a pottery studio where they make beautiful ceramic objects. These are the kinds of activities that come with no urgent agenda. These are the family rituals that we can establish to help us unwind, relax, and enjoy each other's company.

Divorce

Every family can find its own way of coming together. Even some divorced couples are able to make peace and spend regular time together with their children. This kind of cooperation between parents can help make transitions from one home to another easier on their children. When divorced couples aren't able to cooperate in this way, however, it can be more challenging to "retrieve" Persephone. If a daughter (and her siblings, if she has them) are going back and forth between two homes—and in many divorced families, this is a weekly occurrence—it can be more of a challenge to stay connected as she makes the transition from one attachment (her father) to another (her mother). Transitions from one home to another add to the challenge of keeping a bond strong. A mother's awareness and understanding of this kind of "attachment competition" will help her to lovingly contain her daughter as she makes this sometimes difficult and weekly adjustment.

ENOUGH IS ENOUGH

We must teach our daughters to be discerning when they hear about "family values," a term that has been co-opted by some for political gain. Every family should have the freedom to articulate their own values and priorities and to reinforce them by spending quality time together. Teaching our daughters to be discerning in this world is important in many arenas, but nowhere does it seem so essential as with the media.

Consider this: according to statistics cited in the extraordinary documentary *MissRepresentation,* our teenage daughters are at their computers, thumbing through fashion magazines, listening to music, zoning out in front of the television, or watching movies for an average of almost *eleven hours* a day. As a child of the 1960s, wired for tolerance and respect for individual liberty, even I have to ask, how is this possible?

My own parents limited our television watching to the weekends, so that we would have time for homework (as minimal as homework actually was way back before worrying about college résumés began in kindergarten) and time together as a family. Although I hated it at the time, eventually I was grateful that they held that line. My husband and I made the even more radical choice of getting rid of our television when Eliza was born. We wanted to raise our girl free of the warped portrayals of women's bodies and women's lives seen on commercial television. We set up a television screen that was only wired for videos, so that we could decide when and what Eliza watched. As a result, she became a devoted reader before adolescence, and she had plenty of downtime, during which she seemed to get restored and reattuned to herself.

I am aware that it would be too radical a move for most families to "kill" their TVs, as some bumper stickers advise. Every family needs to make its own best choices and to set its own best limits based on its values and what the family members can live with comfortably. But many parents who would hold some line for their kids' future selves may feel, as I do, that a conscious choice must be made about setting a healthy framework of media time (or "up time," as we might call it), family meals, and respectful communication. The earlier we set this healthy frame for our children, the better, because it becomes much tougher to influence our kids when they are teenagers. If they have already become used to a way of life that reflects our values in childhood, it will make our job easier through adolescence. But it is never too late to walk our talk.

Demeter's determination can be our model for fighting for a close relationship with our adolescent daughters, and it can also be our model for fighting to keep the dangerous messages and images of the mainstream media to a minimum. Because of our daughters' precarious position at the edge between worlds, it is we who must teach them to be discerning about the negative, oversexualized images of women that are coming at them every day. I believe we must fight so that our daughters can grow up as confident people in a media-saturated world that undermines them as leaders of their community and of their world. With the following statistics, *MissRepresentation* gives us the sobering reality of the percentage of women who are currently in leadership roles in different sectors of American life:

- 17 percent in politics
- 23 percent in academia
- 16 percent in business
- 18 percent in law
- 11 percent in military
- 12 percent in sports
- 16 percent in film and TV
- 21 percent in the nonprofit sector
- 16 percent in business

Apparently, a girl's peak age for leadership ambitions is eight years old, and it starts to go downhill from there! Does this leave us any room for hope?

Yes! Nine out of ten teenage girls have not totally rejected the idea of being leaders.[1] We mothers can choose to help our daughters rise above the statistics—or more to the point, to change them. We can teach our daughters to take media breaks, to focus on their passions instead of on their appearance. We can be role models for them and for their friends and teach them to use their voices to create change online and off. And we can encourage them to not be afraid to step into leadership roles, since the media is giving them disturbing and extremely confining messages about who they can and can't become in this world.

If our daughters respect us and are primarily taking their cues from us, they will be far less likely to be part of the hook-up-for-sex culture that surrounds them. Sadly, there's a good chance that our teenage daughters are reading about this oh-so-casual sex; hearing about it in music and from friends; seeing it in movies and on television; and yes, maybe even joining in. We need to help our daughters protect their bodies and their hearts. We need to teach them that they are in over their heads if they buy into the cultural BS that sex can be a recreational sport with no emotional involvement. Our daughters (and our sons) are at physical and emotional risk if their peers are their primary teachers about how to be in a sexual relationship. And just as instilling our values in our children is most effectively done by starting before adolescence, so is talking about sex.

Talking About Sex

If we're not talking to our daughters about sex, reproduction, pregnancy, and birth control before they become adolescents, it will be more challenging (okay, awkward) to talk with them when they become teenagers. If we are able to talk openly with them early on, it will feel more natural to them later. From the start, then, you are teaching them that sex is normal, natural, and nothing to be embarrassed about. Although the lines of communication about sex are best opened before adolescence, it is never too late to start talking. If your teen daughter resists, keep talking! If you feel awkward about talking about sex with your daughter, don't be hard on yourself. You can give her the best books on women's health, depending on her age: for example, *The Care and Keeping of You* for preteens and *Real Bodies* and *Our Bodies, Ourselves* for older teens. You can also take her to a women's health-care provider, who will help you educate her.

Am I making you anxious? I certainly felt anxious when my Persephone was in the underworld, dating boys. What relieved my anxiety the most was the strength of our bond. With this strong bond, I knew that I could trust her to talk with me and to tell me the truth. I knew that she knew that I would not judge her regarding any of her sexual behavior. Talking with her about the wide world of sexually transmitted diseases and unwanted pregnancies reduced both of our anxieties, as open communication and accurate information always do.

Here is the reality: A mother (or a father) cannot prevent a daughter from being sexual. If Persephone wants to go into the underworld and experiment sexually, she will find a way to do it. That's the honest truth. So here is where we mothers come in: study after study shows that the earlier kids get clear and accurate information about sex from concerned and nonjudgmental adults, the more likely it is that they will have sex later than their peers and not participate in hook-up-with-no-emotional-commitment sex. And the more sex education teenagers receive, the fewer teen pregnancies there are.

When your relationship with your daughter is close and intimate, you can have intimate talks with her about intimate subjects. You can talk with her about the pleasure of sex—what it is to make love in a loving and committed relationship. A safe and secure bond with you will help her imagine and then manifest a safe and secure bond with another—a bond that one day soon (or *not* so soon) may include sex.

I do understand that sexual relationships are a very complex topic and that it is extremely challenging for us mothers to know how to navigate this territory with our daughters, especially if our mothers did not talk with us about sex—or if they talked *too* much with us about sex! Your motherly intuition will be the crucial tool here to assess what your own daughter needs and where the boundaries between you and her begin and end. I am also not recommending that you talk with your daughter about your sex life—she can certainly see what intimacy and tenderness look like by the way you and her father or your partner show your love through physical affection. Just by witnessing tender touch and kissing between two adults, she can learn a lot about the emotional intimacy that should be part of a sexual relationship.

Talking About Money

Some mothers find that money is as charged a topic to talk about with their teen girl as sex! Where do I begin with such a huge topic? We want to give our daughters everything they need and many things that they want, but many of us don't have the money to do this. It is a tough thing to have to tell our girl, over and over again, that we do not have the financial resources to buy the cool designer jeans she wants or to send her to the amazing summer camp that would broaden her horizons.

Research has shown that nothing negatively affects our ability to parent well as much as financial strain. Nothing. They say that money can't buy happiness, but it can sure buy basic security, which is worth everything, including the possibility that one could be happy in life. If a mother does not have financial security, it will be very hard for her to find her inner resources to parent well. Reading a book such as this one and learning about the skills of mirroring and containing would, indeed, be a luxury. The psychologist Abraham Maslow's famous hierarchy of human needs puts these basic needs at the foundation of his visual pyramid: food, water, shelter, warmth, safety, stability, and freedom from fear. Only when these needs are met can we mother to our full potential.

Although you may not be struggling with poverty, you might be struggling with your sense of value and identity in the workplace versus your value and identity as a mother. Why do the values of these roles need to be compared or prioritized? You may feel torn between your responsibilities at work and your responsibilities as a mother—I know I have been. And American companies are famous for disregarding the fact that you might be a parent and have a family life. Capitalism has put many of us in the impossible position of choosing between work and family in terms of our priorities and our values.

How do we break it to our girls that there is a gender pay gap and that they will likely be making 78 cents on the dollar compared with their male counterparts working in the exact same job? African-American and Hispanic women will earn 62 and 52 cents on the dollar, respectively, compared with their white male coworkers. How might we teach them to fight for their value, financially and otherwise, especially if we haven't been able to do the same for ourselves? There are too many questions and not enough answers here, though some answers may lie in our "emotional financial inheritance"—the mostly unconscious beliefs about money and value that we have inherited from our parents, and in particular from our female role model, our mother. The more we shed light on these inherited beliefs about money, the more we might be free to live our *own* life, financially speaking.

Both my parents grew up in the Depression era, and this had a huge impact on their relationship to money. Understandably, they were never able to totally shake the fear that was instilled in them at that time—that money is scarce—and this has made them both very fearful about and very frugal with money. I grew up with a constant awareness of their anxiety about money; in my family, there was more tension around money than anything else. It has been important for me—especially as a woman and a mother in our culture—to know my value, to achieve financial autonomy, and to pass this on to Eliza. My mother did not have this, as was true with so many women of her generation; they depended on men financially, and a man's work was considered more valuable than a woman's work at home as wife and mother. These are beliefs that I have inherited and that I am still trying to shake, so that I may know, without a shadow of a doubt, that all work is valuable.

As the wonderful organization Girls Inc. states in their Girls' Bill of Rights: "Girls have the right to prepare for interesting work and economic independence. Girls Inc. recognizes that every girl should possess the skills, knowledge, and confidence she needs to achieve financial independence and take charge of her life."[2] Another way that they say this to girls is: "A man is not a financial plan."[3]

Wonderfully, it is through doing work that she feels passionate about (our Mothering & Daughtering workshops) that Eliza has been able to make money and have a taste of what it is to be financially independent. Like her mother, she is a natural entrepreneur, and I can mirror and mentor her in our shared endeavors. How can you mentor your daughter in achieving financial autonomy, even if you have not achieved this yourself?

Discipline

Having a close relationship with your daughter makes it so much easier to talk about loaded topics, such as sex and money. A safe and secure bond with your adolescent daughter will also limit the need for discipline. When the lines of communication are open and there is mutual trust and an easy rapport between you and your girl, her inappropriate behavior can be dealt with in the context of your strong relationship. Consider this: We don't need to punish our spouse or partner or good friend when they have behaved badly; in fact, this would backfire and damage the relationship. Why should it be any different with a teenager? When any relationship has the mutual trust and respect that comes with a strong bond, there isn't much you can't talk about and work out. I am not suggesting here that you treat your daughter as an equal, because you are still in charge. Instead, I am suggesting that you treat her with *equal respect* as you process what might have gone wrong with her behavior and as you figure out how she is going to put the correction in. Your daughter's misbehavior is a rupture, and when you repair it with her, it can strengthen your bond.

Mothering & Daughtering is a relational and developmental approach to parenting, not a behavioral approach. For instance, if your daughter does not call you from a party when she said she would, then you need to get to the bottom of it. Is grounding her going to help? In the long run, grounding will only change the behavior if it is a means through which you improve your relationship with your daughter. In other words, the time at home being grounded could be spent talking or doing a project around the house together. We can retrieve Persephone without punishing her.

The problem with punishment is that it can make our daughters feel further isolated from us, as well as feeling bad about themselves. If time spent grounded means time spent alone in her room, actively *not* talking to you, it's not going to change her behavior or improve your relationship. When your daughter has done something wrong, your goal needs to be to get to what might have *caused* her behavior—not to punish the behavior. You might tell her that she needs to stay home to regroup with you and her family, to slow down and rethink her behavior. You might try to find out whether there was a need driving the behavior. You might ask her if she was feeling pressure from her peers or a desire to fit in. When you probe with love and without judgment, you might find out that she feels deep remorse or even embarrassment or shame. She also needs to know how her behavior may have caused a lot of distress and worry on your part, that her choice has had an effect on you and others. Tears and apologies and a resolution are likely to ensue. This approach takes time and patience, but it is an investment well worth making, for it pays off in the long run. This is a relational approach to discipline. As Gordon Neufeld put it, if we don't "have our child's heart" we cannot parent effectively.

YOUR FAMILY'S VALUES AND VILLAGE

Every family has its own limits and its own way of setting limits. Amy Chua—mother, author, and law professor—created quite a stir with the publication of her book *Battle Hymn of the Tiger Mother*. Her guide to what she calls the "Chinese mother" approach to raising her daughters touched a real societal nerve, provoking a flood of response from readers and reviewers. Ironically, I don't criticize her insistence that she be at the center of her daughters' lives, but I am wary of her almost complete focus on their achievements and her devotion to work without much play.

I am loath to criticize other mothers. For most of us, mothering well is our highest priority, and we are all trying to do our very best. This *Tiger Mother* controversy led me to do more reading on the subject, and I found an article by the controversial philosopher Peter Singer that resonated with me. He states:

> We might take our cues from elephant mothers instead of tiger mothers. Tigers lead solitary lives, except for mothers with their cubs. We, by contrast, are social animals. So are elephants, and elephant mothers do not focus only on the well-being of their offspring. Together, they protect and take care of all the young in their herd, running a kind of daycare center.[4]

I am all for the pursuit of excellence, but I also feel that we mothers need to teach our daughters to find a balance in their lives. We might also seek to be elephant mothers who look out for our whole "herd" of daughters (and sons), so that we might help all of them, in whatever way we can, to pursue their own version of excellence.

My husband and I went out of our way to create an extended family—a village—for Eliza that would provide adult friends, mentors, and teachers who would look out for her. Combined with our will to make this happen—plus quite a bit of luck—we succeeded. We were committed to finding alternatives to the Internet and the mall to occupy her when she was looking for fun. We also wanted her to be part of a "daycare" community for teenagers and not be raised solely by us. Just as friends and mentors helped "raise" her, so too did we watch out for and "raise" their kids.

Although your daughter's peer relationships are not part of the village that raises her (hopefully not!), they are, nonetheless, a big part of her village. One of the things that my husband and I discovered along the way was that our strong bonds with Eliza meant that she gravitated toward other kids who were also close to their parents. Since she thought it was "cool" (relatively speaking) to be close to her mom and dad, she tended to make friends with kids who also liked hanging out with their parents. (This had a wonderful outcome: our adult-looking-out-for-your-kid social net was enlarged!) And I will never forget what Eliza said to me when she was fifteen and dating her first serious boyfriend: "Mom, Johnny is really close to his parents, too!" When you and your daughter have a close relationship, it helps set the bar high for all of her other relationships, including those with her peers. Eliza made loving (and lasting) friendships with her peers during her teen years, and I know that a good part of this was due to the strong bonds she had with her dad and me.

As mothers and fathers do, we looked for what our little girl loved to do, and it was dancing! What we found in our community was not just a dance class, but a dance institute devoted to teaching children dance traditions from all over the world. Her love for and involvement in world dance has remained strong to this day.

We also found a summer theater camp near our home that Eliza loved from day one. When I asked my eleven-year-old daughter that first summer what she loved about this camp, she replied, "I love it because I can be myself. There is no pressure to be cool like there is in school." I thought I had died and gone to heaven. What I appreciated most about the camp counselors (who were mostly in their twenties) was the emotional intelligence they modeled for Eliza. Their lived lessons in empathy and inclusiveness reinforced our family values. I also appreciated that they were not peer-oriented in the least; these young adults celebrated and welcomed friends and mentors of all ages and included parents in most of their events.

I realize how lucky my husband and I were to find two creative communities that helped us raise our daughter. But there are many ways to create a village that includes adults who will watch out for and mentor your daughter. *The Mother-Daughter Project* is an excellent book that can provide you with the necessary guidance to form your own mother-daughter group. Written by two mothers who had success in creating their own mother-daughter group that met regularly, they help the mother reader create a group—a safe haven—with many "village" mothers who are there to help raise each other's daughters.

There are also many excellent afterschool programs that can support your girl by providing a venue for meaningful activities. Girl Scouts, Girls Inc., Girls for a Change, sports teams, jobs, and volunteer internships all can provide cooperative, social environments that reinforce *your* family's values. As parents, we can be proactive in helping our children find a summer community or an afterschool community that is run by adults who we respect, that involves our kids in a passion, and that provides a respite from academics.

I believe that we can and should fight for our daughters' successes, but not in a survival-of-the-fittest manner. Are we going to teach our daughters that climbing the ladder to the top is the only way of measuring success? Are we going to buy into the notion that there is only one kind of intelligence, one that is measured by an IQ test or a performance at Carnegie Hall before they reach college? All of our daughters need to know that their unique talents matter. They need to know that they can and will discover their talents at different rates, and with the help and guidance of their parents and the other adults in the village we create for them.

In the PBS documentary *A Girl's Life*, author and mentor of adolescent girls Rachel Simmons follows four contemporary teenage girls from very different socioeconomic backgrounds through parts of their teen years. Each of the girls meets a significant challenge—cyberbullying, the temptation to be part of a violent gang, being the first in an immigrant family to attend college, body-image issues—over the course of these years. In every case, it is with the help of concerned, involved, and loving adults from their families or their "villages" that these girls successfully make their way. With mothers, fathers, or mentors who help them discover their unique talents, all of our daughters are that much more likely to blossom and to thrive.

SLOW MOTHERING

Just as we are challenged to find out-of-school activities that will help our daughters thrive, we are also challenged to help our daughters keep these same extracurricular activities to a minimum—even though everyone else seems to be doing anything but. The Slow Movement, from which the term and philosophy of "slow parenting" was born, inspired me to trust my intuition and to help Eliza chose consciously and carefully from too many afterschool options. The movement, which advocates a cultural shift toward slowing down life's pace, began in 1986 with a protest against the opening of a McDonald's restaurant in Rome. This protest sparked the creation of the Slow Food (as opposed to fast food) Movement, which advocates savoring slow, convivial meals that feature local farm food whenever possible. Slow "foodies" inspired many to slow down in other areas: Slow Living, Slow Travel, Slow Cities, and, yes, Slow Parenting.[5]

Slow movements have sometimes been misunderstood to recommend that our lives should wind down to a snail's pace. Slow movement advocate Carl Honore (author of *In Praise of Slowness: How a Worldwide Movement Is Challenging the Cult of Speed*) insists that just as there is a *right* speed for snails, there is a right speed for humans—a speed that does not interfere with human bonds. This right speed implies quality over quantity. It allows us the time for real and meaningful human connections and encourages us to be present and in the moment. Honore insists that we allow ourselves the time to remember that child rearing is not a cross between a competitive sport and product development. It allows us the time to appreciate that a daughter's life is a soul's journey, not a project for us to manage.

Eckhart Tolle uses two terms that describe the kind of attention a parent can use with a child: *form-based* attention and *formless* attention. Form-based attention happens in the world of "doing," where many of us mothers find ourselves more often than we would like. In form-based attention, we are telling our toddler to beware of the hot stove, we are telling our middle schooler that we have to leave right now to be on time for her music lesson, and we are asking our high schooler to finish her chores. We are organizing our daughters' lives, and sometimes overorganizing them. According to Tolle, form-based attention is the attention we give to our daughters in our *role* as mother. It goes without saying that a certain amount of form-based attention is essential.

And yet, our daughters' need for formless attention is just as essential. Slow parenting is about giving more of this kind of attention. Mirroring is formless attention. Sharing a quiet moment with your daughter is formless attention. Walking and talking in nature, with no goal except to *be* together, is formless attention. This kind of attention can get lost in the shuffle, but it's worth your while to find it again and again, because formless attention feeds the soul.

When we slow down and remember to provide plenty of formless attention, as well as form-based attention, we might naturally *connect* with our kids before we *direct* them. At this slower, more attuned pace, we might *listen* better to our intuition and *trust* it more easily as it guides us to simplify schedules and clear away clutter. With fewer distractions, we might remember that a slower "earth" rhythm, the rhythm to which our ancestors moved, is always available underneath our overscheduled lives. To find this rhythm, you might want to consider your life like a vehicle that you are consciously putting on cruise control and setting *below* the speed limit. You can always find this earth rhythm in nature. When we get outside and bring our daughters with us, we naturally slow down to listen to the birds and, yes, to smell the flowers—together.

Perhaps no one is more dedicated to encouraging parents to get outside into the natural world with their kids and smell the flowers than Robert Louv, acclaimed author of *Last Child in the Woods: Saving Our Children from Nature-Deficit Disorder.* Louv has named one of his initiatives No Children Left Inside, and he has helped create an organization with the sole purpose of encouraging and supporting the people and organizations that work nationally and internationally to reconnect children with nature. Louv believes—and there is research to back this up—that the more high-tech we become, the more nature we need.[6] Time in nature may indeed be the antidote to one of the epidemics of our time: attention deficit disorder.

A recent study of children from the ages of six to twelve (not an adolescent sample, I realize) showed that, on average, children spend eight hours less per week playing outdoors than their parents did.[7] And although parents in this study reported that 96 percent of their kids have played video games, far fewer (61 percent) had gone hiking. In *Last Child in the Woods,* Louv recommends nature activities for kids and families that aren't just focused on this younger age group. Many activities could be appealing to our adolescent daughters, including the following:

- Maintaining a birdbath
- Viewing nature as an antidote to stress (children and parents feel better after spending time outdoors, even if it is your own backyard or a park in the city where you live)
- Reviving old traditions, such as collecting lightning bugs at dusk and releasing them at dawn
- Taking a hike with your daughter
- Planting a garden
- Raising butterflies (one of Eliza's favorites!)
- Collecting stones, shells, beach glass, and fossils

Like so many recommendations I have made, it is always easier to introduce these activities in childhood and make them a regular part of your daughter's life. But it's not too late to introduce these activities in adolescence or, for that matter, in your adult life. For instance, have you ever maintained a birdbath? Maybe there's an earth mother in you.

Demeter is the first earth mother and our inspiration. She is the goddess of the seasons and the goddess of nature's rhythms. She is the original slow mother who knew what was most important: her relationship with her daughter. She had the power to return her daughter to the safety of their bond, and she welcomed her daughter's comings and goings in the years to come.

And so do you. When you doubt this—because you most surely will doubt your capacity to keep guiding your daughter, again and again, to the safety of your shared bond—remember that you have all the human powers you need to succeed. When you start to feel that keeping her close would require the power of an Olympian goddess, bear in mind that each positive action you take will make a difference and that you just need to do the best you can every day; you don't need to be perfect. Remember that this leg of the journey, the one before your rapidly evolving daughter becomes your more stable adult daughter, is likely the most difficult one, and it will not last forever. Remember that your intuition comes through the instrument of your human body. Your heart beats steadily and loves fully from within that container. And in the end, your perfectly imperfect human self has all the power and determination that you could ever need to keep your mutual bond strong and enduring.

NOTES

CHAPTER 1: A DAUGHTER'S INSTINCT

1. Terri Apter, *Altered Loves: Mothers and Daughters During Adolescence* (New York: St. Martin's Press, 1990), 65.
2. Attachment Parenting International, "API Principles of Parenting," attachmentparenting.org.
3. Apter, *Altered Loves,* 18.
4. Attachment Parenting International, attachmentparenting.org.
5. Apter, *You Don't Really Know Me: Why Mothers and Daughters Fight and How Both Can Win* (New York: W. W. Norton & Company, 2004), 33.

CHAPTER 2: A DAUGHTER'S INHERITANCE

1. Daniel Siegel and Mary Hartzell, *Parenting from the Inside Out* (New York: Tarcher, 2004), 102.
2. Siegel and Hartzell, *Parenting from the Inside Out,* 132.
3. Thomas Lewis, Fari Amini, and Richard Lannon, *A General Theory of Love* (New York: Vintage, 2001), 177.
4. Lewis et al., *A General Theory of Love,* 187.
5. Marion Woodman, *The Pregnant Virgin: A Process of Psychological Transformation* (Toronto: Inner City Books, 1985), 108.

CHAPTER 3: A MOTHER'S INTUITION

1. Mona Lisa Schulz, *Awakening Intuition: Using Your Mind-Body Network for Insight and Healing* (New York: Harmony Books, 1998), 30.
2. Schulz, *Awakening Intuition,* 318.
3. Christiane Northrup, *Women's Bodies, Women's Wisdom: Creating Physical and Emotional Health and Healing* (New York: Bantam Books, 1994), 105.

CHAPTER 4: MIRRORING A SOUL

1. Courtney E. Martin, *Perfect Girls, Starving Daughters: The Frightening New Normalcy of Hating Your Body* (New York: Free Press, 2007), 1.
2. Martin, *Perfect Girls, Starving Daughters,* 5.
3. Woodman, *The Pregnant Virgin,* 16.

4. Rachel's Blog, rachelsimmons.com, January 12, 2012.

5. C. G. Jung, *The Development of Personality: Papers on Child Psychology, Education, and Related Subjects,* trans. R. F. C. Hull, vol. 17 of *The Collected Works of C. G. Jung* (Princeton: Princeton University Press, 1954), 74.

6. Woodman, *The Pregnant Virgin,* 59.

CHAPTER 5: INSIDE EVERY MOTHER IS A DAUGHTER

1. Christiane Northrup, *Mother-Daughter Wisdom: Creating a Legacy of Physical and Emotional Health* (New York: Bantam Books, 2005), 440.

CHAPTER 6: DEMETER'S DETERMINATION

1. MissRepresentation, "Education," missrepresentation.org.

2. Girls Inc., girlsinc.org/about/girls-bill-of-rights/.

3. Girls Inc., girlsincwestchester.org.

4. Peter Singer, "The Human Race Needs Elephant Mothers, Not Tiger Mothers," *The Guardian,* February 13, 2011.

5. Carl Honore, *In Praise of Slowness: How a Worldwide Movement Is Challenging the Cult of Speed* (San Francisco: HarperOne, 2005).

6. Children and Nature Network, "C&NN Initiatives," childrenandnature.org.

7. Children and Nature Network, "Research & Resources," childrenandnature.org.

Resources for Mothers

ACTIVISM FOR MOTHERS AND DAUGHTERS

Do It Anyway: The New Generation of Activists, by Courtney E. Martin. Inspiration for the overwhelmed Millennial generation.

Feminist.com was originally a website for second-wave feminism, and is now also expanding into third-wave feminism. We have a Mothering & Daughtering column on this site.

Feministing.com is a fantastic third-wave feminism site.

MissRepresentation (DVD, 2012). Go out and buy one for yourself and your daughters and sons. (Then buy ten more to give to your friends!) This may be the most important documentary that you and your (older teenage) daughter will ever watch.

Race To Nowhere by Vicki Abeles and Jessica Congdon. This film is a call to challenge current assumptions on how to best prepare the youth of America to become healthy, bright, and contributing citizens. The film provides a lifeline to stressed out teens.

Rookiemag.com is an online magazine for teenage girls with a different theme each month.

Vday.org is a global movement to end violence against women and girls worldwide.

ATTACHMENT PARENTING

Hold On to Your Kids: Why Parents Need to Matter More Than Peers, by Gordon Neufeld and Gabor Maté. This is the best parenting book I have read.

The Myth of Maturity: What Teenagers Need from Parents to Become Adults, by Terri Apter. More great information on why we need to stay close to our teenagers.

BODY, FOOD, AND WEIGHT

Body Drama: Real Girls, Real Bodies, Real Issues, Real Answers, by Nancy Amanda Redd. For older teens; my favorite body book with great information and inspiring photos of real bodies.

The Body Project: An Intimate History of American Girls, by Joan Jacobs Brumberg. A must-read for understanding the history of how we, as a culture, have become obsessed with the shape and size of our bodies.

Brave Girl Eating: A Family's Struggle with Anorexia, by Harriet Brown. Extraordinarily helpful guide for parents of a girl with anorexia.

Eating in the Light of the Moon: How Women Can Transform Their Relationship with Food through Myths, Metaphors, and Storytelling, by Anita Johnston. A beautiful book about healing and emotional eating told through story and metaphor.

The Good Body, by Eve Ensler. A powerful and uplifting play about healing body obsession, by the awesome author of *The Vagina Monologues.*

Help Your Teenager Beat an Eating Disorder, by James Lock and Daniel Le Grange. If your daughter has an eating disorder, I would recommend that you start with this book.

Outsmarting the Mother-Daughter Food Trap: How to Free Yourself from Dieting—and Pass On a Healthier Legacy to Your Daughter, by Debra Waterhouse. This book is really useful in helping to heal any matrilineal inheritance of poor body image.

Perfect Girls, Starving Daughters: How the Quest for Perfection is Harming Young Women, by Courtney E. Martin. Written by an articulate Millennial generation author who helps us understand the "frightening new normalcy" of body hatred. Highly recommended.

Preventing Childhood Eating Problems: A Practical, Positive Approach to Raising Kids Free of Weight and Food Conflicts, by Jane Hirschmann and Lela Zaphiropoulos. This book is the classic on raising children free of dieting.

Teenage Beauty: Everything You Need to Look Pretty, Natural, Sexy and Awesome, by Bobbi Brown and William Morrow. A sane introduction to natural beauty and makeup.

Women, Food, and God, by Geneen Roth. This book is about emotional eating being the doorway to a spiritually lived life. Oprah has called it her "bible" for listening to the wisdom of the body and stopping dieting forever.

BRAIN SCIENCE AND MIRRORING

A General Theory of Love, by Thomas Lewis, Fari Amini, and Richard Lannon. This is one of my favorite books ever. A classic on the neuroscience of the relational, limbic brain.

Parenting from the Inside Out: How a Deeper Self-Understanding Can Help You Raise Children Who Thrive, by Daniel J. Siegel and Mary Hartzell. Wonderful information on mirroring and the basic neuroscience of parenting.

BULLYING

Odd Girl Out: The Hidden Culture of Aggression in Girls (revised and updated edition), by Rachel Simmons. Buy the newly revised and updated edition for chapter 10: "Helping Her Through Drama, Bullying, and Everything In Between." This is a great chapter for parents on how to communicate with your daughter about aggression and bullying, and how and when to intervene.

CELEBRATING MENARCHE

Moon Mother, Moon Daughter: Myths and Rituals that Celebrate a Girl's Coming-of-Age, by Janet Lucy and Terri Allison. Ideas for coming-of-age rituals.

My Little Red Book, edited by Rachel Kauder Nalebuff. This book is a fantastic compilation of first-period stories from women and girls of all ages.

CONTAINERS FOR MOTHERS

Broken Open: How Difficult Times Can Help Us Grow, by Elizabeth Lesser. The appendix has an awesome "toolbox." She offers some of the best information I have found on developing a meditation practice, on finding a psychotherapist, and on working with teachers, healers, and prayer.

EMOTIONAL INTELLIGENCE

Being Perfect, by Anna Quindlen. Inspiring read, for both mothers and daughters, on living life more authentically.

The Feelings Book: The Care and Keeping of Your Emotions, by Lynda Madison. For preteens and teens.

Girls Inc. Presents: You're Amazing!: A No-Pressure Guide to Being Your Best Self, by Claire Mysco. Recommended for all teens.

I Am an Emotional Creature: The Secret Life of Girls Around the World, by Eve Ensler. Fictional monologues and stories inspired by girls around the world. For mothers and older teens.

Raising an Emotionally Intelligent Child: The Heart of Parenting, by John Gottman, Joan Declaire, and Daniel Goleman. This is a guide to teaching children to understand and regulate their emotional world.

GIRLS' AND WOMEN'S HEALTH: PUBERTY TO MENOPAUSE

The Care & Keeping of You: The Body Book for Girls, by Valorie Schaefer. This book for preteens answers questions about body changes, healthy eating, and hygiene, but not sexuality.

Cycle Savvy: The Smart Teen's Guide to the Mysteries of Her Body, by Toni Weschler. An excellent introduction to empowering older teens to watch for the signs of their cycles.

Our Bodies, Ourselves for the New Century, by The Boston Women's Health Book Collective. This classic was essential to me as a young woman, and now this new edition is available for us and for our daughters.

The "What's Happening to My Body?" Book for Girls: A Growing Up Guide for Parents and Daughters, by Lynda Madaras. A great book for preteens and teens about puberty and sexuality.

The Wisdom of Menopause: Creating Physical and Emotional Health During the Change, by Christiane Northrup. The veritable bible of women's health in menopause.

Women's Bodies, Women's Wisdom: Creating Physical and Emotional Health and Healing, by Christiane Northrup. The veritable bible of women's health.

HEALING THE FEMININE

Addiction to Perfection, by Marion Woodman. At the root of eating disorders, substance abuse, and other addictive and compulsive behaviors, Woodman sees a hunger for spiritual fulfillment. It is the cultivation of feminine attributes that heals.

Coming Home to Myself: Reflections for Nurturing a Woman's Body and Soul, by Marion Woodman and Jill Mellick. In this book, 365 of Woodman's core teachings have been formatted for daily contemplation.

Conscious Femininity: Interviews, by Marion Woodman. A wonderful place to start with Marion Woodman.

Goddesses in Everywoman: A New Psychology of Women, by Jean Shinoda Bolen. A very useful guide to understanding female archetypes in everyday life.

Marion Woodman: Dancing in the Flames (DVD, 2011). A breathtaking documentary of Marion Woodman's life and work.

Marion Woodman Foundation: mwoodmanfoundation.org.

The Pregnant Virgin: A Process of Psychological Transformation, by Marion Woodman. "The woman who is a virgin (psychologically and metaphorically speaking) is one in herself; and she does what she does not for power or out of a desire to please, but because what she does is true."

Untie the Strong Woman: Blessed Mother's Immaculate Love for the Wild Soul, by Clarissa Pinkola Estés. A book about the Great Mother, in her myriad manifestations.

Warming the Stone Child, by Clarissa Pinkola Estés. A CD about how to discover and heal the unmothered child within.

HEALING WITH YOUR MOTHER

I Am My Mother's Daughter: Making Peace with Mom Before It's Too Late, by Iris Krasnow. If we, as daughters, can learn to understand our mothers before they die, then we, as mothers, can help our daughters understand us, while we are still living.

Motherless Daughters: The Legacy of Loss, by Hope Edelman. An extraordinary book about the myriad ways that losing a mother can affect almost every aspect and passage of a woman's life.

Returning to My Mother's House: Taking Back the Wisdom of the Feminine, by Gail Straub. Straub beautifully memorializes her mother's unfulfilled life and discovers her feminine self in the process.

INTROVERSION AND EXTROVERSION

One of a Kind: Making the Most of Your Child's Uniqueness, by LaVonne Neff. A helpful book about how to use the Meyers-Briggs Type Indicator as a tool for parenting children with different personality types.

Quiet: The Power of Introverts in a World That Can't Stop Talking, by Susan Cain. I strongly recommend Cain's book—especially her chapter on raising an introverted child, titled "On Cobblers and Generals: How to Cultivate Quiet Kids in a World That Can't Hear Them."

INTUITION

Awakening Intuition: Using Your Mind-Body Network for Insight and Healing, by Mona Lisa Schulz. The veritable bible on intuition.

LEADERSHIP FOR GIRLS AND WOMEN

Eileen Fisher Leadership Institute: eileenfisherleadershipinstitute.com. A transformational summer leadership program for high school girls.

The Girls Leadership Institute: girlsleadershipinstitute.org. Rachel Simmons's institute has a summer camp, yearlong trainings, and seminars around the country for empowering girls to live from their authentic selves.

How Great Women Lead: A Mother-Daughter Adventure into the Lives of Women Shaping the World, by Bonnie St. John and Darcy Deane. A mother-daughter team interviews women leaders and discovers commonly held values, behaviors, and attitudes.

Omega Women's Leadership Center: eomega.org/omega-in-action/key-initiatives/omega-womens-leadership-center. The OWLC is catalyzing a new way of envisioning women's leadership. OWLC is dedicated to redefining power, from "power over" to "power with."

MONEY

Lost and Found: One Woman's Story of Losing Her Money and Finding Her Life, by Geneen Roth. With irreverent humor and hard-won wisdom, Roth offers radical strategies for how we can change the way we feel about money and how we relate to it. This book is also about how to value our deepest self.

Prince Charming Isn't Coming: How Women Get Smart About Money, by Barbara Stanny. This classic guide teaches women how to take control of their own finances.

MOTHERS AND DAUGHTERS

Altered Loves: Mothers and Daughters During Adolescence, by Terri Apter. Invaluable research and reading on mothers and daughters during adolescence.

B, by Sara Kaye. Short, touching, and lovingly illustrated, this is a poem that celebrates the mother-daughter relationship.

How Great Women Lead: A Mother-Daughter Adventure into the Lives of Women Shaping the World, by Bonnie St. John and Darcy Deane. A mother-daughter team interviews women leaders and discovers commonly held values, behaviors, and attitudes.

The Mother-Daughter Project: How Mothers and Daughters Can Band Together, Beat the Odds, and Thrive Through Adolescence, by SuEllen Hamkins and Renee Schultz. This is a fantastic guide to creating an ongoing mother-daughter support group. Invaluable.

Mother-Daughter Wisdom: Creating a Legacy of Physical and Emotional Health, by Christiane Northrup. A remarkable feat of depth and breadth regarding all stages of the mother-daughter life cycle.

Outsmarting the Mother-Daughter Food Trap: How to Free Yourself from Dieting—and Pass On a Healthier Legacy to Your Daughter, by Debra Waterhouse. This book is really useful in helping to heal any matrilineal inheritance of poor body image.

The Red Tent, by Anita Diamant. In this fantastic novel, the biblical culture of women is reimagined as close and strong.

Traveling with Pomegranates: A Mother and Daughter Journey to the Sacred Places of Greece, Turkey, and France, by Sue Monk-Kidd and Ann Kidd Taylor. This is a lovely memoir, written by a mother and daughter, about their journey visiting sacred sites of the Feminine.

You Don't Really Know Me: Why Mothers and Daughters Fight and How Both Can Win, by Terri Apter. In many ways, this is an abbreviated version of *Altered Loves,* so it is an excellent quick read for both mothers and daughters about how conflict can strengthen the mother-daughter relationship.

NUTRITION

Food Rules: An Eater's Manual, by Michael Pollan. Every home should have this definitive compendium of food wisdom.

In Defense of Food: An Eater's Manifesto, by Michael Pollan. This is a manifesto for our times about what to eat, what not to eat, and how to think about health.

PARENTING IN A DIGITAL WORLD

Hold On to Your Kids: Why Parents Need to Matter More Than Peers, by Gordon Neufeld and Gabor Maté. The latest edition has two excellent chapters devoted to parenting in the digital world.

Odd Girl Out: The Hidden Culture of Aggression in Girls (revised and updated edition), by Rachel Simmons. Read the excellent chapter titled "Raising Girls in a Digital Age."

SPIRITUALITY

Are You There God? It's Me Margaret, by Judy Blume. Recommended for preteens.

Broken Open: How Difficult Times Can Help Us Grow, by Elizabeth Lesser. Highly recommended read for help getting through dark nights of the soul.

Creating a Life: Finding Your Individual Path, by James Hollis. This is a rigorous guide to understanding and walking the path of individuation in the second half of life. Highly recommended.

The Feminine Face of God: The Unfolding of the Sacred in Women, by Sherry Ruth Anderson and Patricia Hopkins. A book about the uniquely feminine aspects of faith.

A New Earth: Awakening to Your Life's Purpose, by Eckhart Tolle. A spiritual manifesto for transcending our ego-based state of consciousness.

The Red Book: A Deliciously Unorthodox Approach to Igniting Your Divine Spark, by Sera Beak. For smart, gutsy, spiritually curious women whose colorful and complicated lives aren't reflected in most spirituality books.

The Seeker's Guide: Making Your Life a Spiritual Adventure, by Elizabeth Lesser. The cofounder of the Omega Institute has created a totally wise and accessible guide for the spiritual seeker.